Make Your Own Backpack
and
Other Wilderness Campgear

Make Your Own
Backpack
and Other Wilderness Campgear

by Hugh Nelson

with illustrations by Dennis Reed

Swallow Press
Ohio Univerity Press
Chicago   Athens, Ohio   London

Published by
The Ohio University Press

ISBN 0-8040-0355-6
Library of Congress Catalog Card Number 80-18583

Library of Congress Cataloging in Publication Data

Nelson, Hugh.
  Make your own backpack and other wilderness camp
gear.

    1. Backpacking—Equipment and supplies.
2. Camping—Equipment and supplies. 3. Do-it-
yourself work.   I.   Title.
GV199.62.N44   796.5′.028   80-18583
ISBN 0-8040-0355-6 (pbk.)

Acknowledgements

The authors would like to thank the people listed here for their assistance in the preparation of this book. Rick and Mary Freed of Freed Studios, Thousand Oaks, California prepared the photos. Linden Moss, Jane Pugh, Jan Campbell, Juli Ausmus, and Joan Pappas acted as models. Ethel Kennedy typed the manuscript. Gary Bloomfield assisted with preparation of the drawings.

Thanks also go to our wives, Linda Nelson and Amy Reed, for patience and forbearance.

Hugh Nelson would like to extend a special thanks to Julian Moody for his encouragement throughout the project, and to Hugo Nelson for the foundation experiences that led to this book.

Table of Contents

Chapter 1   Why Make Your Own?   1
Chapter 2   Tools and Techniques   5
Chapter 3   Materials   9
Chapter 4   Sleep Pad   21
Chapter 5   Daypack/Stuff Sack   25
Chapter 6   Sleep Hood   31
Chapter 7   Wind Pants   35
Chapter 8   Insulated Booties   41
Chapter 9   Sleeping Bag   47
Chapter 10   Stuff Sack for Sleeping Bag   59
Chapter 11   Gaiters, Low and High   65
Chapter 12   Mitten Shells   71
Chapter 13   Down or Synthetic Fill Vest/Jacket   77
Chapter 14   Tent   85
Chapter 15   Poncho/Tent Fly/Shelter-Half   97
Chapter 16   Weekender/Soft Pack   109
Appendix I   Suppliers and Kit-Makers   127
Appendix II   General Materials Suppliers   129
Appendix III Fabric Suppliers   131

Chapter 1
Why Make Your Own?

Wilderness hiking is, in part, an attempt to live independently of man's mechanized world. Since the hiker's biological needs dictate that he carry much of his "life-support system" along, he cannot totally divorce himself from man-made gadgets; nor does he wish to. Instead he aims to need as little equipment as possible. Every extra ounce of weight diminishes his appreciation of the surroundings he comes to experience. More important, it is the essence of the sport to accomplish much with little.

If those few required items of equipment are fashioned by the hiker's own hands, the image is complete. He can "taste the freedom of the mountaineer" more deeply than one dependent on others for his gear. In this sense, making one's own backpacking gear is an extension of backpacking itself.

This book is intended to guide those who wish to try making their own backpacking equipment. The items described vary in difficulty and in commitment—in dollars and in time—demanded of the maker. All the projects have been planned to satisfy three criteria: simplicity of construction, light weight, and low cost. Also, they are arranged in approximate order of increasing complexity to help build skill and confidence if sewing is new to you.

Many backpackers spare no expense when it comes to equipment. As in any sport, these "big spenders" justify themselves by claiming reasonable fear of breakdown of inadequate equipment (certainly warranted by some of the junk on the market today). Others may claim they lack the time to comparison-shop for bargains, to make their own, or to hunt for adequate used equipment. It's true that the money spent for high-quality equipment has created stiff competition among many manufacturers and thus promoted the rapid advance of technology in the form of new designs. Both of these results have benefitted the sport over-all by making better equipment available in all but the lowest price ranges.

Unfortunately, this burgeoning market has squeezed the backpacker-on-a-budget mightily. I hope this book will present a viable and enjoyable alternative to the hiker who would like to make his own camping gear—of modern design—inexpensively.

In both buying and making gear, it is vital that one avoid shoddy, undependable materials and construction. Since the backpacker is "unbuffered" from his environment, an equipment failure can become a life-or-death emergency all too easily. On the other hand, given readily-available materials, the novice sewer can construct tough, reliable gear that will provide years of trouble-free service. The value of making your own gear, however, goes well beyond the dollars saved or the security you feel in gear you can trust. Let me elaborate.

My first backpacking experiences occurred while I was in school on the East Coast. The joy of these summer trips and the frustration of the long, cold winters without them (combined with the tedious hours of bookwork) constituted *my* exquisite agony. My first full-time job, in the same area, left me with what seemed to me epochs of free time, and I began to recover by making things—working with my hands. I tried wood carving, drawing, picture-frame making, boat building.

As I got around to making a few bits of backpacking gear, I discovered that several interesting things were happening. First, I was no longer unhappy that it was winter. The cold and snow even encouraged me and challenged my skill to design winter camping gear. Also, the number of things I could make seemed to grow with each completed project, as did my confidence in my ability to use the simple tools I describe in this book. Finally, I got tremendous satisfaction from making these bits of gear; they were useful and often looked as good, if not better, than those I could purchase. Even more important, I could see that the cost of adding necessary gear to my kit was much reduced: it means a lot to be able to think of one's hobby as *saving* money rather than costing money.

Beyond the immediately obvious benefits lay a whole host of other, more subtle, ones. Most important of these perhaps was the ability to *modify* equipment to my specific needs. Many of the items I made at first were adapted from commercially available designs that were not quite right for me. They were too heavy or too light, unnecessarily over-strengthened or too flimsy for backpacking. They were too warm, or coated where I wanted breathable fabric, or made with down where I knew it would disintegrate with ordinary use. Making my own gear permitted me to overcome these inadequacies.

Somewhat later I noticed that my attitude toward my equipment had changed. I began to think of my kit as a collection of valuable but not irreplaceable things. Having made them, I knew their capabilities and limitations. I treated them with respect, for I knew the work that had gone into making them, but I no longer worried about them, as I knew what was required to repair or replace them. This change has had a profound effect on my enjoyment of hiking and camping. It is almost as if equipment worries had been a barrier to the experience of wilderness travel. This barrier had now fallen for me.

Finally, there is the warm glow of "I made it myself" on my gear. With time, each item I've made gets even more deeply embedded in my memory of past trips. It takes on the patina of age. I am more inclined to repair than replace it, which is an environmentally sound practice, anyhow. When something is damaged or worn beyond repair, I am challenged to make the replacement *better* for my use than the original had been.

The satisfaction derived from making your own backpacking gear may be further enhanced in the years to come by the security it provides against equipment theft. Although I have heard only two or three reports of theft of backpacking gear from wilderness campsites, this unfortunate occurrence may well become more frequent as gear rises in cost and hikers become more numerous. Your own personalized equipment, unusual in design, fabric, color, and pattern will discourage most thieves planning to "fence" or sell stolen items. Your name, address, and telephone number prominently displayed in paint or dye on the item (not on a removable name tag) will provide further insurance. Try tie-dye or batik to work your name artistically into the outer shell of your sleeping bag. Make it attractive and colorful and distinctively yours: no one else could stand the constant reminder that it's stolen.

So let me recommend, for all these reasons, that you try your hand and make your own. The rewards are many, the costs few, and the time is well spent.

Chapter 2
Tools and Techniques

Tools

The Sewing Machine

All the projects in this book can be made with a straight-stitch home sewing machine and the simple tools that are available in most households. I have tried to indicate in each of the projects where zig-zag machines and other fancier tools can be used to advantage. In general, though, the straight or curved seams required to make most backpacking gear are easily done by almost anyone on a straight-stitch sewing machine. A modern machine is so simple and safe that a rank amateur can learn enough in fifteen minutes of instruction to begin on the first projects in this book. A straight-stitch sewing machine may be purchased new (see *Consumer's Reports*) or used, or rented for a small monthly charge. Few other tools are required, and careful shopping can bring their cost down considerably. Many are common household items and will find service after you complete the projects in this book.

Pins

Straight pins are vital to even the simplest sewing project. If this is your first attempt at sewing and you fear that you may suffer from "the clumsies," relax. Anyone who has ever tied a fly on a fishing leader or sewn on a button will find machine-sewing a breeze, and will have little trouble with straight pins. For the really ham-handed a special T-shaped seamstress pin is made. Buy a box of two hundred of either type to allow for inevitable loss (Dritz).

Needles

An assortment of hand and machine sewing needles is handy, although a large and a small one of each type will suffice (sizes 8 thru 5 for hand sewing, and sizes 11, 14, and 16 for your machine).

A special "tool" you may find useful is a draw-string threader—a large-eyed, long needle with a blunt end. It will save many tiresome minutes when adding or replacing drawstrings on stuff sacks, elastic in cuffs, etc. Make it from a straight piece of coat hanger wire. With pliers, grip the coat hanger at a bend; flex at this point until the wire fatigues and breaks (or cut it with a wire cutter). Repeat, saving a straight piece about four inches long. Use the pliers to form a loop or eye in one end of the wire: shape is not important, but all snags should either be filed smooth or turned harmlessly inward. The other end should be filed smooth, rounded by adding another smaller eye, or blunted with a drop of glue or solder (Fig. 2-1). A large safety pin is a good temporary substitute for this tool, especially for short drawstrings. A commercial model is available in most fabric stores.

Measuring Tools

One or two yardsticks are invaluable for measuring fabrics on the larger projects. Use rubber bands to create a "five-foot stick" from two yard sticks, for convenience on the tent and sleeping bag. A one-foot rule is equally indispensable for small projects (a clear plastic style has many advantages). Finally, a tape measure will be needed for measuring yourself.

Scissors

You will need a dressmaker's shears. Do not skimp here: They should be of fine steel and sharpened occasionally. The larger projects require considerable amounts of cutting, and there is no faster road to frustration than dull shears. Wiss is a good brand;

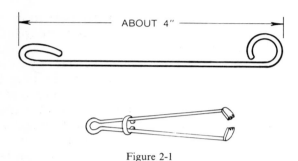

ABOUT 4"

Figure 2-1

probably Sears, too. A small embroidery scissors is invaluable for ripping seams.

Marking Tools

Chalk and a washable marking pen always seem to get some use. Marking pens differ in their ability to write on waterproof fabrics, so take a sample when you shop.

Candle

A candle is handy for fusing synthetic fabric edges, though matches will do for small work. An unusual alternative was suggested in an early issue of *Backpacker Magazine*: A reader made a fabric fuser by propping a soldering iron between two aluminum-foil-wrapped bricks and adjusting the tip height to achieve the proper temperature.* For sleeping bags and tents this rig is almost a necessity. A cheap 30-watt soldering iron costs very little.

Sewing Techniques

I strongly recommend that you swallow your pride and ask some sewing sage for a bit of instruction before you borrow, rent, or buy a sewing machine. Every model has its eccentricities, and even an accomplished sewer can be stumped by an unfamiliar machine.

If the sewing machine, whatever its age, seems ill-inclined to do what you ask, either check the local library for *Sincere's Sewing Machine Repair Guide* or take it to a local repair shop and learn what ails it. Often it is thread tension that strays from adjustment, and any interested sewer can learn to correct this problem easily. Similarly, after a period of use, it is wise to clean and oil your machine. Preventive maintenance is inexpensive insurance.

---

* Idea suggested in a letter by Melvin Dyck published in *Backpacker* #6, Summer 1974.

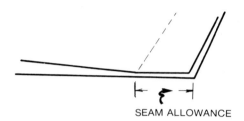

SEAM ALLOWANCE

Figure 2-2

Sewing through several thicknesses of heavier-weight nylon duck fabrics can put some stress on a finely-tuned device like a modern sewing machine. So, be sensitive to its sound and feel in use. On the other hand, don't be deterred from asking much of your sewing machine. New ones are now guaranteed for twenty to twenty-five years of service, which is far longer than most other household appliances. It would almost take intentional sabotage to seriously damage a modern sewing machine.

The standard seam allowance is 5/8" on most commercial clothing patterns (Fig. 2-2). Being a nonconformist, I have deviated quite often from this standard, so watch carefully for seam-allowance figures as you work on the projects. The needle plates of most sewing machines have guidelines that permit you to keep any seam width easily. Check yours, and add a piece of tape if no guide is provided.

Pinning requires planning. In most cases, if two pieces are to be joined, their "right" sides must be together and pinned every three to six inches, so that the bulk of the fabric can pass to the *left* of the needle (sewing head) mechanism (Fig. 2-3). Large pieces passing to the *right* of the sewing head can easily get snarled, in the way, or even sewn into the seam unintentionally. Occasionally, it is possible to sew simple straight seams without pins. Try it after some practice—it really saves time. Rarely will basting be necessary—basting is a long, slow process of hand-sewing pieces together in preparation for final machine-sewing. Hand-basting is much loved by the

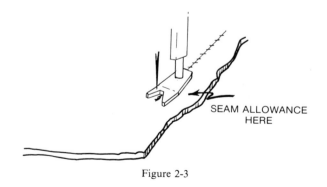

SEAM ALLOWANCE HERE

Figure 2-3

nimble tailor and seamstress, but don't let them foist it on you, novice, unless you care more about "proper technique" than about presentable results in the *near* future.

Reversing the direction of machine stitching at the end of a seam (called back-stitching) is a handy, quick means of tying off, and prevents seams from unsewing themselves. Backstitching is necessary only on seams that will not be crossed or stitched over later on in the project.

Hemming is sewing a raw edge of fabric into a fold so that it is not exposed to abrasion and ravelling. Most hems require a 5/8″ fold back and a seam 1/8″ from the raw edge. An especially fancy hem requires refolding of the raw edge as in Fig. 2-4.

Nylon fabric will melt when heated (and will also burn unless treated—more on this later). This property solves the problem of ravelling edges on fabric. When a cut has been made in nylon (especially taffeta), before any further handling of the cloth, lay it with 1″ to 1 1/2″ overhanging a straight table edge. Singe slightly with a candle flame, being careful to leave no unaffected areas, and especially, to avoid melting a recess in the seam allowance. Blow out any nylon fires immediately! A glass of water should be kept at hand to douse any possible conflagration and save

the project, if all else fails. Again, practice on a scrap until you are fairly consistent. Nylon releases strong fumes upon burning, and adequate ventilation should be used.

When you begin to sew a seam, it is best to trap the two thread ends (one from the spool, and one from the bobbin) under a finger to prevent backlash knotting of the bobbin thread. This is necessary, since light nylon is nearly incompressible and will not bind the thread well until several stitches have been completed.

Choose a fair-sized piece of scrap and sew some long hems, reversing at the ends, until you get used to the machine and the fabric. Do this each time you change to a new fabric, as different fabrics can feel and act quite differently in the machine (in particular, knits tend to squirm and stretch in a usually controllable manner).

Throughout the book reference will be made to the "figure eight" knot shown in Figure 2-5. The diagram should help you learn to tie it.

After some practice, put your tools in order, order some fabric, and you are ready to go!

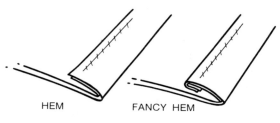

Figure 2-4

Figure 2-5

7

Chapter 3
Materials

Fabrics

Satisfactory lightweight camping gear must be made of quality materials. The selection of appropriate fabrics and hardware is the first task confronting those who wish to make the projects described in this book. This chapter is an attempt to help the novice become acquainted with the materials available and their advantages for various applications.

The presentation is necessarily brief. If you encounter a particular problem of selection not covered here, I suggest you copy the solution adopted by any of the high-quality commercial gear manufacturers. Their experience with field-tested equipment warrants your trust; and their catalogs are a cornucopia of gear-making information.

Nylon

Nylon has been the fabric chosen for most backpacking gear both by commercial manufacturers and do-it-yourselfers. It is cheap, strong, light in weight, and widely available. It is suitable for many applications, and it can be purchased in a variety of weights, weaves, finishes, and colors. Nylon has a built in "give." When stretched beyond its (small) elastic limit, it irreversibly deforms. This feature is advantageous to the hiker in two ways. First, nylon threads can be woven more tightly than fibers with no stretch such as cotton and dacron. A tight weave is essential to the plastic coating processes that are used in raingear, and causes uncoated fabric to have low porosity, that is, to act as a barrier to wind. Second, an item of nylon camping gear, if over-burdened (for example a tent fly in a strong wind), will be more likely to stretch out of shape, and retain some usefulness, than tear. The disadvantage is that a torn item is easily repaired with a few stitches or a patch, while a badly deformed one

must be replaced at trip's end. However, such extreme stress is infrequent in occurrence and can usually be avoided by the careful backpacker.

Lightweight nylon suitable for backpacking gear is available in two weaves: taffeta and ripstop. Taffeta is a plain, non-textured weave with approximately equal numbers of warp and weft threads per square unit. All threads are the same size. It is claimed that taffeta is more abrasion-resistant than ripstop of equal weight, though nylon is generally considered to have poor abrasion resistance compared to cotton. Taffeta may be bought "rough" or in a heat-treated, slick (wet look) finish. It is available in weights of two to four ounces per square yard.

Ripstop nylon is woven of fine threads for light weight—every 3/16″ to 1/4″ a pair of heavy threads are woven into both warp and weft. A hot surface treatment called calendering is given to almost all ripstop fabric. It melts the threads together somewhat. The resulting reinforced web distributes puncture and tear stress to the stronger threads, stopping rips; hence the name. Lightweight taffeta and ripstop can be woven so tightly as to be "down proof"—a desirable property for making down-insulated clothing and sleeping bags. This last property, however, is irrelevant to makers who use other insulators, such as Fiberfill II and Polarguard. These and other synthetic fills are adequately contained by most loosely-woven fabrics. Ripstop nylon is available in weights of from 1.5 to 3 ounces per square yard. Ripstop and taffeta lend themselves to a wide variety of uses for backpacking gear. Both fabrics are now available with a flame-retardant treatment which should be considered for tent and sleeping bag projects. The following list is by no means all-inclusive but only suggestive of some typical applications:

Tents: roofs, doors

Sleeping bag cover: tops

Sleeping bag: outer and lining

Clothing: all types except rain gear

Bags and Sacks: sleeping bag stuff sacks; miscellaneous stuff sacks (but not recommended for packs)

Sleeping Pad: top

Gaiters: linings

Taslan is a nylon fabric specially treated to resemble cotton poplin. The treatment makes the resulting fabric dull and flat in feel and appearance, eliminating the shiny, plastic look of calendered ripstop and taffeta nylon. In other respects it resembles other nylon fabrics. It is most often used in three to four ounce material for making parkas and ski wear and for lamination in making Gore-Tex fabric.

Heavier uncoated nylon fabrics are available in weights from six to eleven ounces per square yard. They have been used for such things as packs, frame pack sacks, canoe sacks, bicycle packs and panniers, gaiters, heavy duty stuff sacks for large items, such as tent poles and sleeping bags. A fuzzy weave called "cordura" is available; it is supposed to be somewhat more abrasion-resistant than the standard flat weave.

Nylon fabric in these heavier weights has essentially no stretch under ordinary use. It is a very tough fabric and withstands much abuse. It should be sewn with double seams (and sometimes with heavy duty thread) so that the seam strength can approach that of the fabric. I urge you to be selective in your use of these heavier fabrics: their strength is not often needed for backpacking applications (except packs) and they add considerable weight when used to excess. Taking care of light gear is often easier than hauling the extra weight of over-built, heavy-duty gear.

Coated Nylon and Dacron

Several companies have developed, patented, and sold rights to waterproof coating processes to be used on nylon fabrics. Nylport and K-kote are notable examples. In past years some of the coated fabrics available lost their coatings through cracking and peeling when exposed to repeated soaking, abrasion, or freezing temperatures. Most of the major name brands have solved this problem, but I must warn the reader that off-brands do exist and may not withstand the test of time and rugged use.

Coated taffeta is probably the most widely-available

waterproof fabric. Its weight (2 to 3.5 ounces per square yard) fits it for the greatest variety of uses. Rain suits, ponchos, pack covers, ground sheets, tent and sleeping pad bottoms, waterproof stuff bags, water hauling bags and buckets, and an assortment of other items can be made with this versatile fabric.

Coated ripstop is also available in a weight range similar to that of uncoated ripstop (1.2 to 3 ounces). Since it is supposed to be less abrasion-resistant than the equivalent coated taffeta, it is generally relegated to use in tent flys, tarps, and rain jackets, which are generally abraded. Except in the very lightest weights, I have found coated ripstop to be just as tough and versatile as coated taffeta in the many applications listed above.

Heavier-coated nylon is generally available as duck or oxford cloth. It is used by manufacturers in packs, luggage, gaiters, overboots, and life-or-death mountaineering gear. Except where absolutely necessary, as in pack sacks, or where weight is less a factor, as in canoe luggage, these heavy fabrics should be avoided in favor of lighter goods.

In several projects in this book I suggest the use of Dacron sailcloth as an alternative to nylon fabric. Excuse my enthusiasm, but I am an ardent advocate of this relatively unused fabric in backpack gear.

Dacron or Terylene (the British trademark) is a fiber with many of the virtues of nylon but no stretch. Fabric woven from it for sailcloth is extremely stiff, and even in the lightest weight (about two ounces per square yard), is not really suitable for clothing (imagine a shirt made of butcher paper and you will understand the problem). Sails must rigidly retain their shape under considerable stress, and tightly woven dacron fills the bill. The stiffness is woven in and lasts for a *long* time—and, unlike the stiffness of new blue jeans, no amount of washing will remove it quickly. This stiffness makes it somewhat more difficult to sew than other fabrics—again, it sews like stiff paper.

If it is no good for clothing and it's harder to sew, what can Dacron sailcloth be used for? It seems to be an ideal pack fabric to me. Since it does not stretch (even in the lightest weights) when it is stitched (especially with Dacron thread), it stays stitched. The stitching in packs receives great stress, and manufacturers have chosen to use heavy nylon in pack sacks to resist the working of seams, their loosening, and eventual failure. Heavy nylon succeeds well when sewn with heavy duty nylon thread; Dacron sailcloth does the same job, but need not be even half the weight of the nylon used for the same pack load. Barring defect, both pack fabrics are far stronger than they need to be for a typical pack load. So it is the "seam strength" that makes the Dacron sailcloth a better choice on a strength/weight basis.

True backpacking fabrics of Dacron are just now coming on the market. A coated Dacron fabric, which will provide all sorts of benefits, should be available soon. These fabrics are presumably more loosely woven and somewhat softer than sailcloth. But since a bolt in the hand is worth several future promises, please consider the benefits of Dacron sailcloth, purchased from a sailmaker or from a yachting supplies store.

Dacron sailcloth is somewhat more expensive than nylon but is more sun- and weather-resistant and may be expected to last longer. It is widely available through mail order, and, in most any large city, it can be purchased directly from a sailmaker. In weight it ranges from two ounces per square yard to twenty ounces or more! The heavier weights are used for storm sails on large ocean cruisers. It is abrasion-resistant and can be heat-sealed along its cut edges, just as nylon can. (It has equally dangerous fumes, so be sure to use adequate ventilation.) It is so tightly-woven and heat-finished as to be non-porous and waterproof with no coating; but like a fine cotton tent, if you touch a roof of it during a rainstorm, it will develop a drip at that point. Thus although it is "waterproof" as a suspended roof, it will not make a waterproof pack or poncho, due to contact on the inside. It is, however, essentially "windproof," as any good sail must be. It also withstands sun and weather for prolonged periods better than nylon or natural fibers.

Again, I must say that Dacron sailcloth is an ideal pack cloth. For both day pack and pack sack use, I feel it's hard to beat, so long as you wear a poncho or hide it inside a plastic bag during a serious rain.

Gore-Tex

Gore-Tex is a laminated fabric that has been steadily gaining popularity for use in weatherproof clothing, tents, and bivouac sacks. An outer layer of Taslan or taffeta nylon and an inner polyester knit layer are laminated to a special Gore-Tex membrane. The membrane is porous to water vapor and, hence, to evaporated perspiration, while impermeable to liquid water.

The theory holds that Gore-Tex fabric is waterproof but breathable, certainly a winning combination for outdoor wear and rainshelter. Neither the fabric-maker nor the manufacturers of Gore-Tex gear claim it as a miracle. They do affirm that the fabric is waterproof, and

that it reduces condensed moisture in clothing and tent applications.

In practice Gore-Tex is subject to leakage from three sources. Body oils "poison" the membrane layer, rendering it permeable to water. Thorough cleaning, per instructions, reduces or eliminates this problem. Gore-Tex, like any waterproof fabric, will leak at seams. Special seam sealants are available for Gore-Tex laminate fabrics. Most Gore-Tex garments are sold with seam sealant included for the purchaser to apply, and perhaps reapply, until satisfactory sealing is achieved. Gore-Tex fabrics are subject to delamination: the separation of the sandwich layers. Since the outer and inner layers provide dimensional stability to the delicate inner membrane, delamination is likely to mean the end of the water-proofness of a garment or shelter.

Other considerations are Gore-Tex's relatively high weight and cost. A parka that weighs 1-1/2 pounds *may* be light enough to be considered backpacking gear if it replaces, say, a waterproof rain jacket and a windproof shell that are normally carried. Garment Gore-Tex weighs about five ounces per square yard, so most commercially made parkas are in the one-and-a-half to two-pound range. At $9 per yard, or $75 to $130 per parka ready-made, I blanch at the thought of toting Gore-Tex gear into the real world of rocks and briar, campfires and mud.

Even given that Gore-Tex really works under some circumstances, I have lingering doubts about its effectiveness in certain situations. When the outer fabric shell is saturated with water from rain, snow, dew, etc., could the inner membrane still conduct vapor? Similarly, how could the laminate retain its breathability when coated with frost condensed on a tent or bivy sack canopy? My experience with Gore-Tex leads me to believe that under these conditions it would act as any coated fabric would act, and that, depending on your expectations, may be acceptable performance.

Cotton-Nylon and Cotton-Dacron Blends

A fabric widely used for mountain parkas and other water repellent applications is 60-40 cloth, Ramar, or stormcloth. This rather expensive cloth is a tightly-woven blend of nylon or Dacron warp and cotton weft, which is porous but wind-resistant and when chemically treated repels water in anything short of a dunking or a prolonged rain. It is of moderate weight (four ounces per yard), suitable for jackets, scree gaiters, strong stuff sacks, etc. It is abrasion-resistant and remarkably water repellent in its new condition. However, the chemical treatment wears, weathers, and washes off in time and should be renewed, perhaps with Scotchguard, which now seems to be available in a spray can without the ozone-depleting fluorocarbon repellent. The mountain parkas available in this fabric seem better suited to standing around at busy trailheads, rock-climbing haunts, or on college campuses than to backpacking: they are just too heavy for their limited usefulness.

Some near relatives of 60-40 cloth are the cotton-Dacron blends sold in most fabric shops, in denim, duck, and oxford weaves. Less important than the per cent fiber composition is the tightness of the weave and resultant wind-resistance, if you are planning to substitute this less expensive cloth for a typical 60-40 cloth use. The stretchy nylon in 60-40 cloth creates a very tight weave that's hard to duplicate in a dacron blend without creating stiffness. The repellency resulting from the "bath" which impregnates the 60-40 fibers is also hard to achieve with Scotchgard spray. If you do not require extreme wind-tightness or water repellency, then try a dacron blend and pocket the difference in cost.

Nylon Netting and Cotton Knit

Two other fabrics are required for the projects in this book, and they deserve brief mention here.

The sleep hood in Chapter 6 is made of cotton T-shirt knit fabric and matching rib-knit. Both these fabrics are widely available but are not likely to be seen in backpacking stores or catalogs. If you have an old but undamaged T-shirt, consider recycling it to make a sleep hood. Since it is never under great stress, it need not be of new fabric.

Nylon netting is used for the screen doors and windows of the tent. It is extremely light in weight and relatively fragile. If you should burn or tear a hole in it, use a match to seal the raw edges and patch with a scrap as with any other fabric. Some manufacturers use nylon net as baffle material in making down sleeping bags. If the down gets wet and the bag is treated roughly, the down can cascade through one or more baffles creating a difficult-to-repair cold spot. Be careful with a wet down sleeping bag.

Tape and Webbing

Waist and shoulder straps, attachment loops, reinforcements, and handgrips on backpacking equipment are usually made of nylon or cotton webbing. Many varieties of webbing are made, including flat and tubular weave, widths from 3/16″ (called lace) to 2″ automobile seat belt width. There are tight, hard weaves and soft, flexible types all in a range of thicknesses and colors to suit most any need.

While there is a great variety of webbing made (especially in nylon), it is sometimes difficult for the do-it-yourself maker to find sources. Thus, you should expect to have to limit your webbing choices to the few standard widths (generally 5/8″, 1″, and 2″) for which buckles and other hardware for backpacking are made. These sizes can be obtained from most major backpacking equipment retailers in one or a few colors and thicknesses. (If you have special requirements, it is well to investigate an awning and canvas shop, a sailmaker, a surplus store, upholsterer, or other potential users of the type of webbing you seek. If possible, get hardware for any odd size webbing when you buy it, since it may be unavailable elsewhere.)

Tape is the designation used for soft thin webbing used for facing hems, etc. If it is of nylon and strong enough, it may be useful to back stressed seams or to reinforce snaps. Heavier webbing or strap fabric finds a multitude of uses in strengthening and providing loops for attachment on backpack gear. Broad cotton strap is certainly strong enough for most hiking applications, but remember its greater susceptibility to mold and mildew and keep it away from moisture, especially damp soil, and also from constant soaking by perspiration. Remember, too, that perspiration is salty: salt-starved back-country rodents can devour handgrips and shoulderstraps and ruin your trip. Rinse them occasionally and the problem will be diminished.

Hardware

Metal parts used on hiking and camping gear should be protected to retard corrosion. Iron and steel parts are generally nickel- or chromium-plated. Brass corrodes very slowly, so corrosion is rarely a problem except in a marine environment; it is also plated with nickel for some backpacking uses. Aluminum forms a tenacious oxide that prevents further corrosion. Since these are the most commonly-used metals on hiking gear, corrosion problems are not generally encountered. Aluminum can cause difficulties, though, if used where it is rubbed constantly by clothing, pack, or other fabric: a dark smudge will appear on the fabric which is difficult to remove.

Buckles

Buckles are used to bind straps, as in backpack closures, shoulder and waist straps, and sleeping bag lashing straps. There are four main types of buckles used on hiking gear. The spring-loaded clamp—used primarily in 1-1/2″ width for waist bands on hip suspension packs (Figure 3-1a). The slide jaw buckle (Figure 3-1b) is also suitable in 1-1/4″ width for waist straps but receives its greatest use in 5/8″ and 3/4″ width for pack-bag closures, lashing straps, snow-shoe bindings, and so forth.

Since both of these buckle types use teeth to dig into the web fabric, they hold securely but do eventually abrade the webbing at the point of most frequent use. These buckles are suitable for most moderate to heavy weight webbing that is not too smooth.

The third type is the tabler buckle (Figure 3-1c.) It has no slide or clamp but depends on friction to secure the strap end. It does less damage to the strap it holds than either of the previous types and is quite easily adjusted. Its disadvantage is that, since it depends on friction for its holding ability, any great change in strap tension or a pull to the side may cause it to slip. It is accepted now as the best possible shoulder strap buckle, because of its "one hand" adjustability, but of limited use otherwise except for lashings. It functions best on relatively "rough" webbing.

A fourth buckle type is the Double D or Figure 8 (Fig. 3-1d.) It is not intended to be easily adjustable, but rather to hold a doubled strap in a semi-permanent and very secure grip. It also depends on friction but is not subject to slippage if the strap tension changes. Its primary use is to hold the webbing end looped through another buckle, D-ring, or snap.

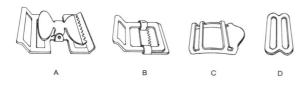

A   B   C   D

Figure 3-1

Snap Hooks and D-Rings

A more secure and somewhat faster-to-operate fastening is a snap hook looped into a D-ring. The system is metal-to-metal and is thus less likely to be damaging to the fabric straps involved. It is found at the lower attachment points of shoulder straps and on "belly bands" (non-weight-bearing waist straps) of climbing and ski-touring day packs. It is also common on military surplus gear. If you are careful to keep the metal parts from areas where they can dig into tender skin or abrade fabric, the combination can be useful.

Hook and Eye

Bent wire hook and eye fasteners can be of use in some backpacking applications, since they are made in a large (and therefore strong) size and nickel-plated. I have suggested the use of the hook-half as a lace hook to hold the high gaiters in place at the lower end of the hiker's boot lacing. Using a long-nose pliers, these hooks may be bent to suit other applications.

Grommets

A grommet is a doughnut-like bit of thin metal that is hammered tight through a hole in fabric to distribute stress applied to the hole and to metal-clad the hole against tearing. There are two materials used to make home-applied grommets: brass and aluminum. Grommets generally use a thin disc of metal called a washer that fits against the wrong surface of the fabric to distribute stress.

The aluminum grommet depends on the spreading and crimping of the clipped side of the grommet tube to hold it tight against the fabric. Brass grommets are more malleable, and the tube lip is spread and rolled when hammered. Both types of grommets work well and are easy to install using only a hammer and the tools provided in the kit. Aluminum grommets are the choice if you have only a few small (1/4″ inside diameter) grommets to install. They are available from Dritz and are sold in most yard goods and variety stores. A small package contains twenty or so grommets, including a tiny but serviceable setting tool. A true bargain.

For larger grommets, or if you plan to do many grommeting jobs, you should consider a grommeting kit for use with brass grommets. These are available from backpacking equipment retailers in sizes "0" and "1" (1/4″ and 5/16″ inside diameters respectively). (Brookstone Company has all sizes cheaper; see Appendix I.) Completely different tools are needed for each size (they are not interchangeable), so grommetting can get quite expensive. The brass-washered grommets look very neat and professional and hold very well, but I have never had an aluminum *or* brass grommet pull out, so I urge you to consider carefully before investing in expensive grommeting tools. Your aim in making backpacking gear is, at least in part, to save money. Note: *Always* use eye protection when hammering.

Eyelets

Eyelets are small unwashered grommets with an inside diameter of about 1/8″. They serve well for drawstring lace holes (for example, on the calf of the high gaiters) and make excellent ventilation holes in hats, jackets, and rain suits. They are set with a pliers-like tool from Scoville that is also used to punch the hole for their placement (other brands are also available). Always be certain to heat-fuse such holes if they are made in synthetic fabrics or they will ravel and the eyelets will pull out.

Snaps

A small, crimped snap called a pearl snap, the kind found on western shirts can be set with the eyelet tool described above. Other snaps, like grommets, can be set with a hammer (Baby Durable, Durable Dot snaps and tool available from Frostline). Sew-on type snaps are available in a variety of sizes (Dritz). Most closures that can be made with snaps can also be made with zippers or velcro, however, so use your discretion. On parkas and gaiters, a snap-closed flap is used to cover and protect the zipper from snow and wind. Snaps are also necessary in securing the sides of a poncho against flapping.

One benefit you may derive from owning snap and grommet tools is just their presence in your work area. Tools have a strange way of stimulating creativity; inventing new ways to use them becomes a part of the whole process.

Zippers

Zippers come in a wide variety of styles and sizes, useful to the backpacker and camper. Nylon zippers are most popular since they cannot freeze closed, are less cold to the touch in a sleeping bag, and presumably more dependable than metal.

A zipper's strength with respect to pull perpendicular to its length is determined by its tooth size. Continuous coil zippers have quite small, weak teeth. Their design prevents snagging of fabrics, an exceptional virtue, and they are unharmed by being "ripped" open by a strong

pull. Separate tooth zippers in nylon (YKK is a typical brand) can be made to separate completely and are very strong in the sizes suitable for backpacking gear (size 5 has 3/32″ teeth; size 10 has 1/8″ teeth). Once "ripped" open, they must be repaired (difficult) or replaced, and they are as susceptible to fabric snags as most metal types.

Finished zippers are available in lengths ranging from tiny 6″ zippers for light-weight clothing application to 106″. By special order or by buying coil zipper by the foot, almost any length is possible.

To obtain zipper lengths other than the standard ones, it is a simple matter to shorten a non-coil nylon zipper. First, zip the zipper together and mark the length desired on the tapes or teeth; then unzip the zipper again. Using a long nose pliers, pry the U-shaped end clamp open enough to remove it from the end of the teeth. Use the pliers to squeeze the zipper tooth just beyond the mark; it will fall off easily when cracked. Place the end clamp in place where the tooth was removed. Repeat these steps for the other zipper end clamp. Zip the zipper and check its length. Then proceed to cut off the zipper tapes 1″ beyond the end clamps, and crack the extra teeth. Zippers are available with different slides and patterns of opening for differing applications. Here are some examples: one end closed, one slide with an outside and an inside pull (suitable for a sleeping bag) or with a double slide for ventilating the feet while the torso stays warm; completely separating, double slide with one pull on each slide (for a parka); closed at both ends, opening in the middle with two slides (for a pack pocket or sleeping bag compartment, as on the Weekender Pack). Many more variations and combinations are possible in the suppliers' catalogs.

Velcro and other Hook/Pile Fasteners

One last type of fastener deserves mention: Velcro. Velcro is a pair of nylon tapes, one fitted with hooks and the other a pile surface on which the hooks snag, much like burrs on a wool sweater. Velcro is available for clothing uses as continuous tapes in widths of 1/2″ to 1-1/4″, or as dots of 1/2″, 3/4″, or 1″ diameter.

Velcro looks delicate, but apparently it is not. In correspondence I carried out several years ago with Frostline, a leading kit manufacturer, they reported that a Velcro strip had been opened and closed 100,000 times with no significant loss of holding power. Velcro is easily sewn in position, requiring no special tools. It opens and closes easily in the dark, in a storm, or a wind, and its strength is proportional to the tape area used. It is light in weight and comes in a variety of colors. It is relatively expensive, but, considering its versatility and the cost of alternatives, worth the price.

Insulating Materials

Insulating material, or "fill," is employed to trap the body's warmth in a layer of dead air space. I have left the discussion of the pros and cons of various fills to the chapter on the sleeping bag, where that information is most relevant. Here I will briefly list the main materials and their uses.

Down

Down, the under-feathers of waterfowl raised in northern climates, is acknowledged to be the loftiest insulation for its weight. Prime goose down exceeds the loft of the best synthetic fills by one third; it is also more compressible and recovers its loft after compression better. Since loft determines warmth, down possesses the highest warmth to weight ratios of all fills. Down's disadvantages are not insignificant, however. Its cost is rather high (check R.E.I. or Frostline catalogues), depending on quality. When wet, down mats and loses almost all of its insulative property; it is difficult to dry. Since down is an animal product, it is subject to mildew and oxidative breakdown in time. Finally, a few people are allergic to down. Duck down has all the advantages and disadvantages of goose down except its cost and loft are relatively lower.

Synthetic Fills

Hollofil II and Polarguard are brand names for two different polyester fibers, the first made by a Du Pont process and the second by the Celanese Corporation. Dacron has been a popular fill for heavy car-camping and canoe sleeping bags in the form of Dacron 88 and Dacron Fiberfill. Bonded Dacron batts have long been used to make quilts, pillows, etc., and this book shows you how to use them to make a serviceable and light mummy sleeping bag. A few years ago backpacking equipment manufacturers began marketing sleeping bags and insulated parkas made with these two new fills—Dupont Hollofil II and Celanese Polarguard. The new substances were developed specifically for lightweight sleeping bags and were supposed to be significantly better in loft-to-weight than previously available synthetics. Dupont Hollofil II is

a short-fibered fill (2″) which must be stabilized by quilting or other method for sleeping bag use. It is soft, waterproof, in that it absorbs almost no water, and has about two-thirds the loft of an equal weight of down. Polarguard is a continuous filament fill, bonded into a running batt by a water soluble resin in manufacture. It needs less quilting to stay in place, since its fibers run the length (or width) of the fill compartment. It is not as soft as Hollofil II but can be made into a lighter sleeping bag. It is supposed to be quite similar to the Dupont product in warmth-to-weight. See Chapter 9 on sleeping bags for a comparison of down and these two synthetics.

Thinsulate

Thinsulate is a fairly new fill material from 3M. It differs from other available fabric insulators in that it maximizes warmth per unit of thickness rather than warmth per unit of weight. In other words, when used in a jacket, eight ounces of down might give an overall loft of three-quarters of an inch and keep one warm at 20°; at the same temperature, perhaps one-half inch of Thinsulate will provide the same warmth with less bulk in a more form-fitting, fashionable garment. The backpacker should note, however, that a one half-inch layer of Thinsulate might weigh twice what the down weighs. Thinsulate finds its best use in applications where low bulk is critical and weight is a minor consideration such as ski wear and other high fashion winter clothes. Thinsulate resembles other synthetic fiber fills in its ability to retain warmth when wet, and to dry rapidly after wetting.

Foam Insulation

There are several firms marketing sleeping bags made of foam—polyether, or polyurethane—or combinations of foam and other fills. I have had no experience with these, so I suggest two books by authors who have each made one inexpensively and described its construction.* I can recommend a polyurethane foam sleeping pad, as described in Chapter 4. The pads are warm and comfortable and make an excellent easy chair for evenings around the campfire.

Polyurethane is the foam used to make mattresses; it is sold in several densities, of which only the lightest is suitable for a backpack sleeping pad. Its color is white

* See Robert J. Kelsey, *Walking in the Wild* (New York: Funk & Wagnalls, 1973); or Paul Cardwell, Jr., *America's Camping Book* (New York: Scribner's, 1976).

when new and yellow when aged, though the aging apparently does not change its properties. For backpacking pads, the 1-1/2" and 2" thicknesses are the best compromise between weight and comfort.

Youngsters and spartan types seem to thrive on hard beds. Closed cell foam makes an ideal sleep pad for them: its closed cell structure prevents absorption of moisture and traps dead air space so well that only 1/4" to 3/8" is required for warm sleep on snow.

Ensolite is the older closed cell foam product. It is soft enough to stuff and yet dense, but it is heavy and fairly expensive. Ensolite's color is "natural tan." A newer closed cell foam of polyethylene is available in a range of colors (blue, black, white), weighs only about one-third as much as Ensolite, and costs only half as much. Polyethylene is a good choice despite several disadvantages: stiffness, greater bulk when rolled up on a pack frame, and more easily torn. The stiffness of the "bluefoam" polyethylene foam is an advantage in the construction of the weekender pack where it is used to pad the back and shoulder straps. (See the June, 1976 [#21] issue of *Backpacker Magazine* for reviews and ratings of trail bed foams.)

Cord, Lace, and Rope

Lace is a narrow form of webbing; it is a flat-woven or braided fabric, 1/8" to 1/4" in width, and usually 1/16" thick. It is useful for clothing drawstrings, light stuff bag ties, etc. Its flat shape holds knots better than round cord, and it packs smaller when stuffed or folded. Lace can be difficult to untie if tightly knotted, however.

Contrary to popular usage, cord is not just small-diameter rope. Strictly speaking, cord is a round braided material, while rope is three (sometimes four or more) yarns twisted into a "rope lay." Large diameter cord consisting of a braided casing over linear fibers (called kern-mantle) is quite commonly used in rock climbing and sailing, while small-diameter cotton rope is sold as package twine.

Rope can un-lay (that is, untwist) when badly treated, and this is a disadvantage to backpackers. Synthetic fiber cord of 1/8" to 1/4" diameter, commonly called parachute cord, is probably the best choice for most camp uses. It is light in weight and far stronger than its natural fiber counterpart. It can be heated with a match to prevent unraveling at the ends. If kept clean and out of the elements when not in use, it will remain strong and last for many years.

One-eighth inch nylon cord is generally rated at 400-500 lb. test. This is strong enough for almost any backpacker's need, including lifting a person in an emergency. I prefer somewhat larger cord, however, for a number of reasons. The weight difference between 1/8" cord and 3/16" or 1/4" cord is very small considering the quantities a backpacker must carry. The larger cord ties and unties much more easily—a real advantage in the dark—and is more visible and less likely to trip someone in dim light. Finally, the larger diameter provides an extra margin of strength if the cord becomes weakened by abrasion, and, being broader, is less likely to cut the hands if used for hauling packs, water, etc.

Nylon cord is the most widely available of the common synthetic fibers. It is inexpensive and the best choice for most hiking uses. Polypropylene and Dacron ropes and cord can be gotten from marine equipment shops and some fishing tackle and hardware stores. Polypropylene comes in a variety of colors and it floats; it is stiff and slippery and hard to knot. Dacron has less stretch than nylon but is similar in most other properties. It is quite expensive, however, and best left for wealthy yachtsmen.

Cord-Locks

The innovative mind of the backpacker has created a "knot" that can be untied with one hand, in the dark, in the twinkling of an eye. It is called a cord-lock. Made of plastic or nylon, it is a spring-loaded tube-within-a-tube that can be "tied" and "untied" thousands of times with no damage to the cords used. There are other designs available so shop before you buy.

Cord-locks are recommended for four projects in this book. The suggested applications are: the hood drawstrings on the sleeping bag; the drawstring tops on the sleeping bag stuff sack, the day pack, and the weekender pack; and the flap tie-down on the weekender pack. An examination of your equipment may reveal other uses for these inexpensive, but versatile, little gadgets.

Water Repellent vs. Waterproof and Seam Sealants

There are several products on the market purporting to make outdoor gear waterproof or water repellent. What are their differences? Can they do the job?

Water repellency is generally accepted to mean that an item or treatment product will shed water in a rain, mist, or fog for a time and retain its ability to "breathe out" the perspiration of the wearer. The protection is less than perfect, however, since the clothing fibers can become saturated. Then the garment becomes sodden—air cannot circulate and rain soaks through readily. Scotchgard by 3M is such a water-repellent treatment; it is also reputed to repel dirt. Tightly-woven cotton, even when not treated, is water-repellent in the sense that a cotton tent canopy or awning will not transmit water through its thickness unless touched inside while wet.

Waterproof is a more specific term. Waterproof fabrics, gear items, and treatment products are intended to be a one hundred per cent barrier to water and, therefore, to air. Polymer-coated nylon (and Dacron) fabrics are remarkably waterproof and yet light enough for backpacking applications. They are used largely for raingear, packs, and stuff-sacks. The waterproofness of these items depends almost entirely on how carefully the seams are sealed, since the fabric is an impregnable barrier to water.

The seam sealants used by backpacking equipment-makers are available to the do-it-yourself maker through their catalogs. Pliobond is a honey-like substance that remains flexible when dry and seals thread and needle holes when brushed over seams. It smells bad and the odor lasts indefinitely. Other sealants (K-Kote, Tite-Seal) and solvents are available; some can be sprayed on seams if you have a miniature paint sprayer. Seam sealants are difficult to apply to all stitching in a pack-sack, hence they are rarely water-tight. For rainsuits, ponchos, and tent flies, the seams are fewer, more accessible, and less stressed and they can generally be made quite waterproof.

It is probably a bad idea to attempt to waterproof a large cotton or nylon fabric area with a rubber or plastic paint-on waterproofing product (such as Flex-Dri). These products are intended for use on canvas and would greatly increase the weight of a backpacking tent, for instance. Make or buy a light, coated nylon tent fly instead, and you will be repaid with a more waterproof shelter and a lighter load.

Thread and Needles

Thread to be used on the sewing machine is widely available in cotton-covered polyester and pure polyester types. Pure cotton sewing-machine thread seems to be a thing of the past, but that's no great loss for the sewer of backpacking gear. These polyester-based threads are much stronger than cotton. I prefer the cotton-wrapped polyester type, since it is supposed to bind to the fabric better in sewing and present a softer surface which is less likely to cut into the fabric. A friend claims that the

European polyester thread that he uses is stronger than what's made in the U.S. I cannot comment, since I have not seen the results, but you may wish to investigate.

Nylon thread is available in the crafts departments of most variety stores. I used it for a while, but found it made an excessive amount of fuzz which collected in my sewing machine. Its stretchiness is reputed to cause more frequent missing of stitches than non-stretchy polyester thread, though I have never had the problem.

At times I have used heavy-duty thread with large (size 20) needles to sew especially thick, rugged gear. My results were disappointing; thread tension was never good and skipped stitches were common. I have abandoned this practice in favor of a moderate size 14 needle, ball point, and standard weight thread (size 50). I double-stitch all seams that receive moderate to heavy stress.

Hand-sewing may be required in some of the projects (especially on packs), and heavy duty thread can add strength in this application. You may even wish to use braided or monofilament fishing line as thread.

Elastic

Elastic tapes and cords can be used to advantage in many items of hiking and camping gear. The most obvious applications are in waistbands and sleeve and cuff closures. Others include use in mittens and gaiters to keep out wind and snow, and as top closures on stuff sacks for such things as cook kits, cameras, tent poles, etc.

I find stiff, tight cuff closures annoying; therefore, I use only lingerie elastic (sold primarily for underwear and pajamas) on clothing items. Whatever strength elastic you choose, its width must be determined by the fabric it is to be used with. Narrow 1/4″ to 3/8″ lingerie elastic will crinkle light nylon ripstop or taffeta as it should, but wider and stronger elastic will be needed to properly fold 60-40 cloth or the mid-to-heavy nylon used for gaiters. For cuff closures using soft elastic, I find an elastic length about ten per cent smaller than the limb (wrist, ankle) circumference to be comfortable. Note: Always allow excess elastic for overlap to complete the loop.

Leather

Leather is employed only sparingly among the projects in this book. Its advantages are great strength with flexibility, abrasion-resistance, and its non-woven composition. Its disadvantages are its weight, cost, and susceptibility to damage by animals and mildew.

Leather adds the look of quality when properly applied to packs, parkas, and other climbing and hiking gear. Its properties recommend its use especially for strap attachment patches and abrasion-resistant mounts for ice axe and crampons on packs, and similar hard-wear points on other gear.

There is really no reason for the leather used on backpacking gear to be brand new. Discarded boots, shoes, moccasins, slippers, jackets, vests, etc. can provide a surprising amount of free leather to the willing re-cycler. Suede is not significantly different from top grain in its important properties, and only the flexibility and thickness of a piece of leather should determine its usefulness in your project.

* * *

I hope the suggestions offered here can add to your equipment-making success. The projects that follow in the next chapters employ these materials to what I hope is their best advantage. An appendix is included at the end of the text listing sources for most of the material items mentioned, with addresses for ordering by mail if you can find no local supplier.

Chapter 4
Sleep Pad

After about one week of trail hiking I am "in shape." Blisters, if any, are turning to calluses; the aches of rarely-used muscles have almost disappeared. I have adapted to the altitude and cooler temperatures of the high country. My pack is lighter and I am stronger. This is the physiological "high" of a good hiking trip.

The first symptoms of "civilized-itis" often strike at this time, however. Rocks and logs and snow seem uncommonly hard. The awe that they inspired early in the trip is replaced by the realization that these are my only pillows and pallets. My mind wanders back to that plush easy chair in the living room and the almost sinful luxury of the sofa in the den. This psychological state, which I call "civilized-itis," is common to all backpackers, I believe. It makes the wise ones doubt their sanity, the soft ones switch from hiking to Mah-Jongg.

One treatment for civilized-itis is to provide yourself a bit of comfort where you sit and lie down. May I recommend the sleep pad described herein when things get "rough."

Materials

Foam:	Dimensions to fit you. See text.
Top Fabric:	Cotton or cotton/Dacron
Bottom Fabric:	2 to 3 ounce coated taffeta or ripstop nylon
Foam Insulation:	1-1/2" or 2" polyurethane foam, light density
Ties:	Two 30" nylon tapes, 1/2" wide

The foam sleep pad is quite simple to make. It requires only a few straight seams, some inexpensive and readily available materials, and a bit of time.

At a hardware, discount, or yard goods store purchase a piece of foam, 1-1/2" thick (2", if you seek real luxury and don't mind the extra weight), no larger than 24" × 54" and no smaller than 20" × 48". The sizes given will make an adequate "shortie" pad for camp lounging and sleeping. A full-length pad is too heavy and bulky for backpacking, and a skimpy 36"-long, shoulder-to-hips pad is just too small for comfort. If you are broad shouldered or long-waisted, lean toward the larger dimensions, but cut the pad size to the smaller measurements if possible to save weight. If you plan to make more than one pad, search for a bargain foam sheet that can be cut into pad-size pieces.

Foam padding of the thickness described cuts easily with a *sharp* carving knife. Mark the lines you wish to cut with a marking pen and straight-edge. Cutting will be easiest if there is someone else who can spread the kerf as you cut with a smooth sawing motion. Avoid a serrated knife edge since it will make thousands of tiny, "clingy" foam chips. Also try to keep the knife perpendicular to the foam to insure square edges and corners.

Theoretically, the polyurethane foam pad, once cut to size, is an ideal mattress. It is insulative against the cold of the ground, and soft against its hard irregularities. It breathes too, allowing escape of perspiration from the hiker's back surfaces.

Practically, however, the pad needs some protection. The breathing property of the foam is a result of its open-cell structure. Sponges, both natural and man-made, also exhibit this open-cell property—and all three materials drink up water . . . like a sponge. Uncovered foam also picks up dirty readily and would quickly soil the user's sleeping bag.

A cover is the solution to these problems. The cover top is best made of non-slippery cotton or cotton blend fabric to retain "breathability" and prevent the sleeper from slipping off his bed. The bottom of the cover should be of waterproof-coated fabric to discourage absorption of puddles and should extend a bit up the sides of the pad. Coated nylon taffeta in two to three ounces per square yard weight is preferred for the bottom, as it is waterproof and fairly resistant to abrasion. The pad top-piece may be subject to your creative urges. Keep the fabric fairly light, non-slippery, and of a color or pattern that won't show the dirt too readily. It could even be tie-dyed, have a checkers or backgammon game board, a group logo, etc.; use your imagination.

Once you have settled on a foam pad size, cut the fabric pieces as follows. The bottom piece is cut 3″ wider and 3″ longer than the foam piece it will cover. The top piece, of cotton blend fabric, is cut the same width as the bottom piece and 7″ shorter. The head piece is also cut the same width as the bottom piece and 12-1/2″ in length (Fig. 4-1).

Construction of the sleep pad is very simple and straight-forward. The first step is to hem the top piece. Fold one short (widthwise) edge of the top piece 1″ toward the wrong side; pin and sew near the raw edge as shown in Fig. 4-1. Sew a similar 1″ hem in one widthwise edge of the headpiece, folding the raw edge to the wrong side (Fig. 4-2).

Cut and heat-fuse the ends of two 1/2″ × 30″ nylon tapes to be used as ties when the pad is rolled.

Now place the bottom piece (non-slick side) right-side-up on a table or the floor. Fold the tapes in half lengthwise and align the fold with the head edge of the bottom piece (Fig. 4-3). Pin. Locate the tapes at one-fourth and at

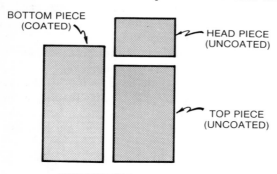

BOTTOM PIECE
(COATED)

HEAD PIECE
(UNCOATED)

TOP PIECE
(UNCOATED)

(SEE TEXT FOR DIMENSIONS)

Figure 4-1

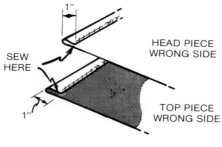

1″

SEW HERE

1″

HEAD PIECE WRONG SIDE

TOP PIECE WRONG SIDE

Figure 4-2

BOTTOM PIECE RIGHT (SLICK) SIDE

ALIGN FOLD WITH EDGE

Figure 4-3

three-fourths of the width of bottom piece. Place the head piece over this assembly right-side-down and align its three unhemmed edges with those of the bottom piece.

Next place the top piece on the other end of the bottom piece, right sides together, and align the unhemmed edges with those of the bottom piece (Fig. 4-4). The top piece will overlap the head piece along their hemmed edges. Pin the top piece in place along the three aligned edges.

Sew around the entire assembly 1/2″ from the raw edges, if you use 2″ thick foam; 3/4″ from raw edges, if you use 1-1/2″ foam. If the top piece is rather loosely woven or seems likely to unravel, zig-zag or straight-stitch over the seam allowances 1/4″ from the raw edges.

Since the corners of foam pad are rectangular, it is a nice touch to make those of the fabric cover fit precisely. This tends to discourage the cover from sliding around the foam block. To put box corners in fabric cover, it is necessary to fold and pin the fabric at the corner so that the top/bottom seams are aligned (Fig. 4-5a, 4-5b, 4-5c). This results in the top fabric being folded on itself, right sides together, and the bottom fabric being folded on itself, right sides together. Locate the corner seam so that its length, 1-1/2″ or 2″, is equal to the foam thickness. Cut away the excess fabric leaving a seam allowance of 1/2″. Repeat this folding, pinning, sewing, and cutting procedure for each corner.

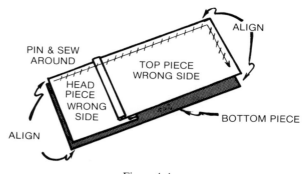

PIN & SEW AROUND

ALIGN

TOP PIECE WRONG SIDE

HEAD PIECE WRONG SIDE

BOTTOM PIECE

ALIGN

Figure 4-4

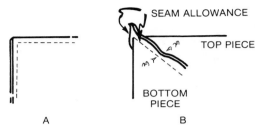

SEAM ALLOWANCE

TOP PIECE

BOTTOM PIECE

A   B

Figure 4-5a & b

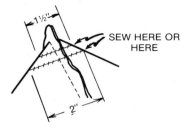

1½"

SEW HERE OR HERE

2"

Figure 4-5c

Invert the cloth sleep pad cover and slide the pad in place inside. Bending the pad along its length will help if it fits tightly. Recline on your creation and admire your work.

In use, a sweater or jacket can be stuffed under the overlapping headpiece to form a pillow that will not slither away during the night.

To roll up the sleep pad, start from the bottom to permit the escape of air and use straps to hold it in place on your pack frame.

Chapter 5
Daypack/Stuff Sack

A strong, light daypack is a pleasure to have along on any but the shortest backpack jaunts, and it is a necessity for day-long hikes, shopping trips, bike rides, and so on. Unfortunately, few commercial products can qualify as *both* strong and light.

The *strong* daypacks are made of heavy nylon duck, often coated with waterproofing, and are built to last. They have zippers, pockets, padded straps, leather patches. They are quite bulky, and hardly qualify as a backpacking tool, since they weigh a pound or more when *empty*. Needless to say, they are priced in accordance with their aesthetic appeal rather than their utility.

The *light* daypacks often come from the Orient. They are made of taffeta, poorly designed—often as deep as a laundry bag—and poorly constructed, with raveling raw edges, loose stitching, and junk hardware. Often they fold into their own pocket. The "working" of lightweight taffeta causes such a bag to rapidly fall apart when even lightly loaded. My first backpack sewing project was such a taffeta daypack. It lasted through about four months of twice-weekly use, often carrying groceries.

Its successor, similar in size, shape, and capacity, and not more than one ounce heavier, has lasted through seven years of similar active use. It has often carried up to twenty-five pounds of groceries and/or books, been taken on scores of backpack and day-hike journeys, and has only recently been awarded semi-retirement—as an emergency bike pack—for its meritorious service. In all that use, no seam has ever needed re-sewing, and only one "battle scar" has needed repair.

I feel certain that the remarkable performance of this pack is attributable to its being made of Dacron sail cloth. This pack fabric has essentially no stretch; neither does the cotton-wrapped Dacron thread it was sewn with. The combination seems particularly strong and abrasion-resistant.

It is this Dacron daypack that is the subject of this chapter. First, some statistics: depth 15″; width 14″; thickness 4-1/4″; volume 1,080 cubic inches; weight 4-1/4 ounces; capacity up to twenty-five pounds (though it's intended for comfort with much smaller loads); rolled-up size: a cylinder 5-1/2″ long by 2-1/2″ in diameter; cost: very low. When used as a stuff sack, it will easily hold a four-and-a-half pound down- or Dacron-filled sleeping bag.

The daypack is intended for day-trip use from a base camp, ski lodge, hostel, etc. It is equally suited for toting sweaters, lunch, and camera on hikes or bike trips near home. Its drawstring top and undivided volume fit it admirably for use as a clothing or sleeping bag stuff sack, thereby eliminating several more ounces from the backpack. It is simple in appearance and construction, and will reward the maker with few envious glances but with many years of dependable service.

Materials

   2/3 yard Dacron or nylon fabric 44″ wide

   Two 11″ pieces of 1″ nylon or cotton strap material

   4-1/2 feet of 1/8″ or 3/16″ cord or lace

   Eight grommets, 1/4″ inside diameter (Dritz Large Eyelets, for example)

   Dacron-and-cotton thread

   Scraps for practice

   One *Cord-Loc* or other cord fastener (optional)

Tools

   Sewing machine, pins, rule, etc.

   Matches and candle

   Iron

Marking pen or chalk

Grommet setting tool (comes in Dritz Eyelet set)

Heat source (gas stove)

Expendable 1/4″ rod, nail, screw, bolt, etc. or soldering iron

Pliers

Hammer and expendable board

1/4″ to 1/2″ dowel or curtain rod

Cutting Out

As with several other projects in this book, the fabric pieces are very simple in shape, and no pattern is required to cut them out. I urge you to acquire some Dacron sail cloth in two to four-ounce weight (per square yard) to make this project, and I promise you will be satisfied with the result. If you choose to make the daypack of nylon, choose duck or cotton/nylon mountain parka cloth.

Cut out the fabric pieces as indicated in Fig. 5-1 and heat-fuse the raw edges.

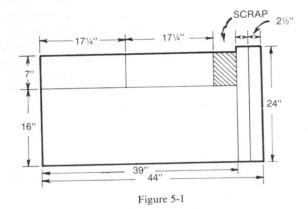

Figure 5-1

Assembling the Bag

The first sewing step is to join the side and body pieces along their long edges. Align the right-hand side piece, right side (rough side, if you are using coated fabric) down, with the edge of the body-piece, and pin 1″ from the edge, as shown in Fig. 5-2. Continue pinning across the bottom and up the other edge of the side piece, making a sharp corner at the indicated dots. Now sew along the pin line. Place another row of stitches just outside this seam (that is, just a bit closer to the raw edges).

Repeat the above procedures for the left-hand side piece.

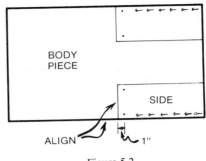

Figure 5-2

Making the Drawstring Top

Next we will add a drawstring to the top of the bag. Fold and press the side-seam allowances toward the body piece. Fold the raw edge of the bag top 1″ toward the wrong side, and press. Now fold this 1″ fold again, 1″ toward the wrong side; pin, and sew with two rows of stitches close to the lower edge (Fig. 5-3).

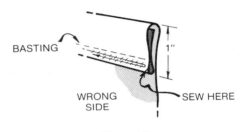

Figure 5-3

This triple layer of fabric will now act as a foundation for the 1/4″ grommets which will hold the drawstring. This grommeted type of drawstring is preferable where there is a large amount of fabric to take up in the closed position.

With a marking pen, space eight dots equally around the drawstring fold to mark the centers of the eight 1/4″ grommets to be used (Dritz grommets work well in this application). With a bit of fudging you can get four grommets to pass through the thick side-seam allowances for extra solidity. Now search for a 1/4″ metal rod (nail, screw, bolt, etc.). Using old pliers and a gas stove, camp stove, or blow torch, heat the rod by holding it in the flame with the pliers until it is hot enough to pass easily through all three layers of the fabric. You may wish to practice on a scrap. Pierce the fold at the eight marked points, insert the grommets, spurred or washered side toward the wrong side of the bag, and hammer them home against a board.

Adding the Straps

The straps are made of the same material as the bag. They are quite strong, have little bulk, and are very light. The Dacron covers a bit of 1″ nylon strap material in the shoulder area, which prevents their becoming wrinkled and rucked.

The strap length given in Fig. 5-1 should fit just about anyone with 34″ to 42″ chest size. If you are particularly large in the chest area or shoulders, longer straps might be advisable, or their bottom attachments points might be raised and spaced further toward the bag sides.

Begin the straps by folding and pressing the strap fabric pieces in half, lengthwise, with a cool iron. Sew 1/4″ from the long raw edge and across one end (Fig. 5-4). Invert both strap pieces over a dowel or curtain rod.

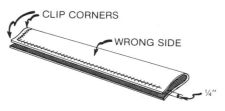

Figure 5-4

Check to see that nylon strap material is heat-fused at both ends, and insert these pieces into position 2-1/2″ from the open end of the Dacron sheath (Fig. 5-5). Stitch the nylon in place 1/4″ from each end.

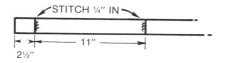

Figure 5-5

Now draw a 1″ × 2-1/2″ rectangle, centered and 1-3/4″ below the top of the drawstring band of the strap side of the pack (Fig. 5-6). Pin the left strap (the strap that will go over the left shoulder) in place (Fig. 5-7), and baste by machine. Fold the right strap piece similarly and baste in place (Fig. 5-8). Now sew these strap ends firmly in place; I suggest a short zig-zag stitch and a pattern such as that shown in Fig. 5-9. Be certain to backstitch over the beginning and end of each seam to discourage the threads from working loose.

The other ends of the straps can now be folded over 1″

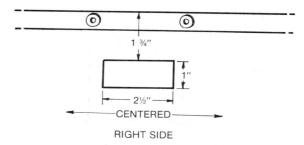

Figure 5-6

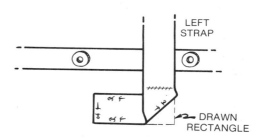

Figure 5-7

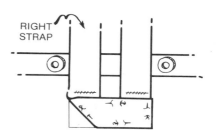

Figure 5-8

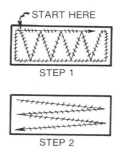

Figure 5-9

and stitched into place at the positions shown in Fig. 5-10. Again, zig-zagging will strengthen this attachment point if your machine has this capability.

27

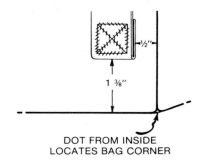

DOT FROM INSIDE
LOCATES BAG CORNER

Figure 5-10

Finishing Touches

If you plan to use the daypack extensively as a stuff sack outside of your backpack, a dust flap would be a good addition. Make it 9″ to 11″ in diameter and attach it to the strap side of the bag, as described in Chapter 10 on the sleeping bag stuff sack. Install a 1/8″ or 3/16″ cord through the grommets, leaving the tails at center back. Add a cord-lock if you wish, then tie a "figure eight" knot in each cord end (see Chapter 5) and your bag is complete.

28

Chapter 6
Sleep Hood

When the sun has set and the campfire burns low, the evening cool descends in the mountains. Weary hikers lower stiff limbs onto soft sleeping bags and pads, finding the exquisite relaxation that only physical exertion can bring.

Early evening temperatures in summer are often too warm for sleep in a closed bag, so many hikers unzip to the waist, or even use the sleeping bag as a quilt for the first few sleeping hours. This leads to another problem, however. At 55°-65° the air chills bare skin so rapidly as to prevent sleep. What to do? There are probably as many solutions as there are backpackers. My cure is a long-sleeve shirt, thin gloves, and the sleep hood described in this chapter. The combination is comfortable enough for sleeping uncovered and can be used again inside the bag in the chilly pre-dawn hours to provide that extra measure of warmth.

Most backpacking how-to-do-it books recommend a stocking cap or watch cap for this application. If you've tried it, I'm sure you have found that it makes your "hair hurt," as it does mine. I can suffer this mild annoyance for one or two nights, but over a week's hiking the pain is too much to anticipate, especially since it is avoidable.

The problem is that the stretchy knitted cap pulled tight over the scalp combines with the tossing and turning of a night's sleep to compress and bend the hair follicles in the "wrong" direction. The solution is the sleep hood—of thin cotton knit—which keeps some warmth in but is loose enough not to make the scalp suffer. It has the further advantage of covering more of the head and neck, being adjustable even to the point of leaving only a small breathing hole for severe cold, or slipped down about the neck in anticipation of cold yet to come. It can be worn under a brimmed hat for chilly hiking days, with the ribbed neck band acting as a scarf. It is also an effective insect shield when dabbed with repellent and will serve to keep the hood of your sleeping bag free of oil and grime that accumulate in the hair.

Materials

12″ × 24″ T-shirt cotton knit fabric
4″ × 20″ cotton rib knit
36″ soft cotton cord
One large sew-on snap set

Begin by washing your cotton fabrics to preshrink them. If you wish, the main hood piece may be cut from an old cotton T-shirt. This will make it light, cheap, and recycled—admirable backpacking virtues—and will eliminate the need for pre-shrinking. Otherwise, choose lightweight cotton knit and ribbing in a fairly conservative color: it's bound to get dirty and will show the dirt less.

You will need a 12″ × 24″ piece of cotton knit fabric for each hood plus a 4″ width of tubular cotton ribbing knit (which is sold in a tube shape, about 20″ in circumference), 1 large sew-on snap set (i.e., 1 male part snap and 1 female part receptacle), and a 36″ piece of soft cotton cord for the face drawstring.

Cut the knit fabric to the shape shown in Fig. 6-1 after folding with right sides together along the line indicated.

Unfold the cut piece and fold the long straight edge "E" 1″ toward the wrong side (Fig. 6-2).

Sew near edge "E", tucking the raw edge under 1/8″ as you sew, and creating the drawstring sleeve.

Now re-fold the fabric piece right sides together as in Fig. 6-3. Sew 1/2″ from the curved edge, then zigzag stitch over the seam allowance near the seam to discourage their tendency to ravel. Henceforth, this will be called the nape seam.

Turn the assembly right side up. Cut the ribbing piece along one of the "ribs" to make a long piece 4″ wide. Fold this ribbing piece along its length and align its raw edges with the neck edge of the fabric piece leaving 1″ of excess ribbing length at each end as shown in Fig. 6-4.

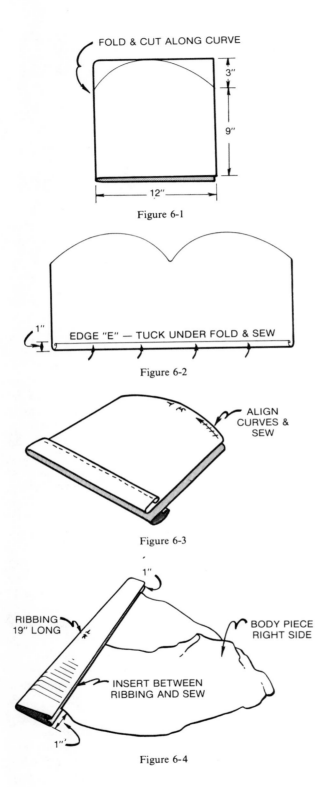

FOLD & CUT ALONG CURVE

3″

9″

— 12″ —

Figure 6-1

1″

EDGE "E" — TUCK UNDER FOLD & SEW

Figure 6-2

ALIGN
CURVES &
SEW

Figure 6-3

1″

RIBBING
19″ LONG

BODY PIECE
RIGHT SIDE

INSERT BETWEEN
RIBBING AND SEW

1″

Figure 6-4

Pin the ribbing in place at the nape seam only. Lower the sewing head at the nape seam and stretch the ribbing and fabric ahead of the needle. Begin sewing, keeping a moderate tension on both fabric and ribbing and aligning the edges as necessary (if your sewing machine has a "stretch stitch," use it here). Continue 1″ past the end of the fabric on the ribbing alone. Turn the assembly 180° and sew from the nape seam to the other end, again sewing 1″ of excess ribbing beyond the fabric edge. Clip a 1/4″ slit at both ends of the drawstring sleeve on the wrong side at a point just above the ribbing seam. With a drawstring threading tool (see Chapter 2), insert the 36″ length of soft cotton cord into one slit and out the other. Center it in the drawstring sleeve then stitch down at the top center of the sleeve with several passes of machine stitching. Tie a "figure eight" knot (See Figure 2-5, Chapter 2) in each cord end.

Now try the hood on and pull the ribbing around your neck till it forms a comfortably snug fit. Mark the place where the end of the ribbing overlaps. Sew the female part of one snap set in place 1/2″ from the mark, closer to center front (Fig. 6-5). Sew the male part of the snap set in a corresponding spot on the overlapping ribbing end.

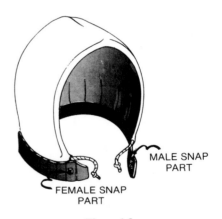

MALE SNAP
PART

FEMALE SNAP
PART

Figure 6-5

The sewn-on snaps are used because of the cold spot that the metal back-plate of a grommet-type snap would create on the wearer's neck.

Your sleep hood is now complete. May it keep you comfortable on many a chilly night. (By the way, there's no reason to restrict its use to backpacking occasions.)

Chapter 7
Wind Pants

The wise backpacker is prepared for worse weather than he expects. This preparation requires careful planning, however, if the burden is to remain light. Rain protection both while hiking and in camp is essential. Extra layers for warmth are equally important. The hiker's greatest natural enemy, hypothermia ("exposure"), thrives on cold weather, wet gear, and exhaustion—and it can be a killer.

A garment that I have found well worth its light weight—and very small bulk—is the wind pants described in this chapter. They function to trap warm air around the legs and have proven their usefulness as an extra layer while hiking in chilly, windy passes, around the campfire, and in the sleeping bag on especially cold mornings. Like a wind-breaker or shell jacket, they do not insulate, but only cut down convective heat loss by reducing air flow. They are not used every day but for the few ounces they weigh and the few dollars to make them, these pants provide light, cheap insurance. They sure feel great on a blustery day and have earned their place in my kit, over and over again.

Commercially available wind pants are a bit fancier than the ones described here, but they are also about twice as heavy and at least twice as costly.

Wind Pants and Rain Pants

I urge you not to make rain pants of this design. Waterproof fabric over the lower extremities will prevent evaporation, and perspiration will accumulate. In time the insulating clothing underneath (pants, long johns) will become damp and, unless you can get to a dry environment or a strong heat source, body warmth will be required to dry these clothes. Rain pants and jacket will make you nearly as wet as the rain they ward off, unless the weather is very cold and you are inactive (sitting in a boat or snow cave). A poncho is far better ventilated and rain chaps may be added for cold, wet hiking.*

Materials

  1-1/2 yard × 44″ light nylon
  7″ non-separating zipper (optional)
  60″ × 3/16″ nylon lace
  Two 1/4″ grommets
  24″ × 1/2″ soft elastic

These nylon wind pants dry rapidly and might serve as emergency rain pants in real cold. They would warm the legs somewhat, even though wet, and the insulative long paints could be stored dry, in the pack, for camp use.

Choosing Fabric and Fitting

Uncoated light ripstop nylon (about 2 ounces per square yard) is probably the best fabric choice for the wind pants, with light nylon taffeta a good alternative. Very dark colors radiate heat well and light ones show dirt readily, so the best choice is a medium color.

If the pattern is laid width-wise on the fabric, 1-1/2 yards of 44″ wide should suffice for hikers up to 6′3″ tall.

Three measurements are needed in order to properly fit the wind pants:

  Inseam Length: Measure from crotch to cuff on a fitted pair of slacks

  Crotch Depth: Sit on a straight back chair and measure the vertical distance from the waist (belt top) to the chair seat

  Circumference: Measure around the body at the belt line.

The pants dimensions given in Fig. 7-1 are related to the

---

* My own solution for hiking in summer rain, cold or warm, is a poncho and short pants. The lower legs are exposed and may get chilled, but the upper body stays warm and dry under a poncho and the general level of miserableness doesn't get too high as long as I keep moving.

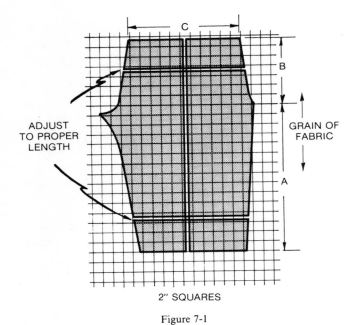

Figure 7-1

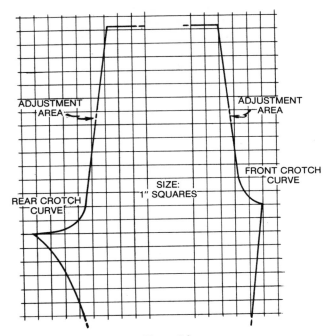

Figure 7-2

above measurements in the following ways (numbers given in parentheses are those for persons over 6'1" in height):

Dimension A is equal to the measured inseam length, plus 3" (4").

Dimension B is equal to the measured crotch depth, plus 7" (8").

Dimension C is equal to one-half the waist measurement, plus 4" (5").

Making the Pattern

The shape of the crotch curves shown in Fig. 7-2 should be traced onto newspaper or special pattern paper available at fabric stores. Use a bright-colored marker to create a 2" × 2" lattice, then transfer the curves square by square.

Cut out the curve patterns and tape or pin them to another piece of newspaper in the positions in Fig. 7-3. Be certain to position the curves so that the Dimensions A, B, and C correspond to the wearer's sizes. Complete the waist edge line and the inseam edges with straight lines and cut out the completed pattern piece.

The crotch curves should be aligned so that the inseam lines converge slightly, giving a cuff circumference of 24". This large cuff permits donning the wind pants without removing the boots.

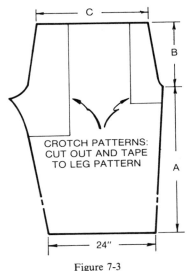

Figure 7-3

Cutting Out

Fold the fabric transversely, lay the pattern in place and pin. Both pieces may now be cut from the fabric.

Installing the Stuff Pocket (Optional)

By adding only a bit more in weight and complexity, the wind pants can be fitted with their own belt-looped stuff pocket. When the pants are being worn, the inverted "sack" doubles as a zippered, carry-all pocket. Note: A similar pocket/sack might be added to other projects in this book (e.g., daypack).

If you choose to add the pocket, cut out the piece shown in Fig. 7-4. Mark the center line as shown with chalk. Purchase a 7" non-separating zipper that matches or contrasts with the fabric you've chosen. A zipper slide with pull tab on both sides is desirable but not necessary.

On one pant leg piece draw a chalk line 10" long, starting 3" from the center rear crotch seam and 3" below the raw waist edge as shown in Fig. 7-5. This pants piece will henceforth be the right-leg piece. Next align the center line of the pocket piece with the chalk line on the right-leg piece and pin along the center-line.

Now sew a 7" by 1/4" rectangle starting 3/4" from the pocket piece edge and 1/8" from the center line. The resulting box encloses the slit to be made through both fabric pieces (Fig. 7-5). Cut the slits and seal their edges with a flame.

Next, tuck the pocket piece through the slit. Topstitch along the edge of the slit to give it a neat rectangular appearance. Place the zipper, closed with tab down (if there is only one tab) on the "pocket side" of the assembly (i.e., so that the zipper tapes rest on the pocket piece) and pin. Sew all around the zipper about 1/4" from the zipper teeth.

Belt loops are now attached to the "zipper tape side" of the pocket piece on the part that extends beyond the waist edge of the right leg piece (Fig. 7-6). The belt loops are made from a scrap strip 7" by 1-1/2". Fold and sew the strip lengthwise and sew across one end. Turn this tube inside out over a pencil. Fold this in half again and sew it lengthwise along both edges (See Fig. 7-7). The resulting strip can be cut into two belt loops, and attached in the position shown in Fig. 7-6.

The pocket is now completed by folding the pocket piece along the zipper center-line, aligning the raw edges and sewing with a 1/2" seam allowance.

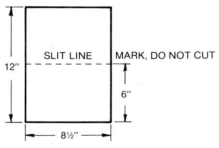

Figure 7-4

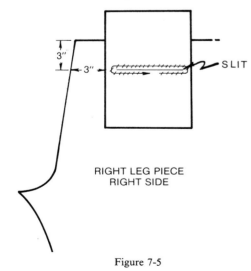

RIGHT LEG PIECE
RIGHT SIDE

Figure 7-5

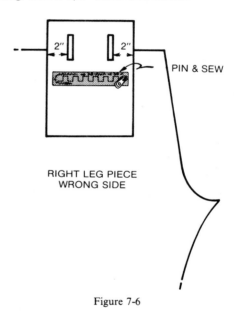

RIGHT LEG PIECE
WRONG SIDE

Figure 7-6

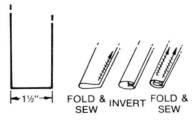

Figure 7-7

Sewing Inseam and Crotch

Fold the right leg piece (the one with the pocket, if you added it) along its length, right sides together (pocket out), and align the inseam edges. Pin. Begin about 1/2″ below the crotch edges and sew this inseam. Repeat the process for the other leg. (Be certain that the right sides are together or you will produce two right legs!) These seams may be strengthened and neatly finished by folding and stitching (felling) the seam allowances, as in Fig. 7-8.

The crotch seam is next and is made quite easy by two tricks. First turn the right leg right-side-out and insert it, cuff-down, into the left leg (which is still wrong-side-out, Fig. 7-9). This makes them concentric; it also brings both right sides into contact along the crotch seam. Align the inseams and pin in both directions up to the waist edges. Second, begin sewing at the inseam, allowing a 1/2″ seam allowance, and sew to the rear waist edges, being careful not to catch the pocket in the seam. Now sew from the inseams to the front waist edges. Again, it is advisable to fell the seam allowance.

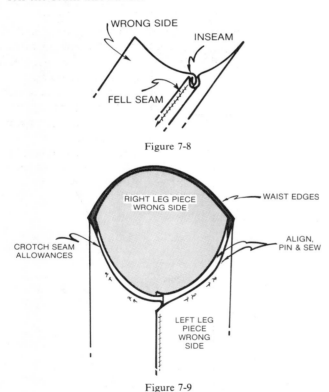

Figure 7-8

Figure 7-9

The Drawstring Waistband

The pants waistband is a tube enclosing a nylon lace. It is made by folding the raw waist edge 2″ toward the wrong side. Press with a cool iron, pin and sew near the raw edge (Fig. 7-10).

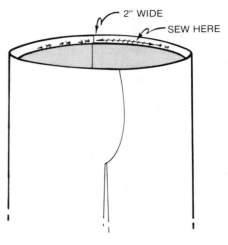

Figure 7-10

At the center front 1-1/2″ below the folded edge, melt two 1/4″ holes through both thicknesses and install grommets as shown in Fig. 7-11. A thin leather or thick fabric patch on the wrong side would help secure these grommets.

The drawstring tube can now be completed by folding the folded edge 1″ toward the wrong side, enclosing the grommets. Pin and sew near the top and bottom of the new fold (Fig. 7-12).

Using the threading tool described in Chapter 2 on tools, insert one end of a 5′ length of 1/4″ or 3/16″ nylon lace (or cord) through one grommet and out the other. Center the lace in the tube and stitch over it a couple times at center back. Try the wind pants on and tie them. Heat-fuse the drawstring lace ends and tie with the bulky "figure eight" knot shown in Fig. 2-5 to prevent their disappearance inside the tube.

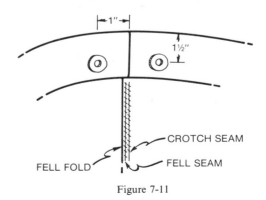

Figure 7-11

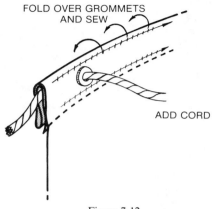

FOLD OVER GROMMETS AND SEW

ADD CORD

Figure 7-12

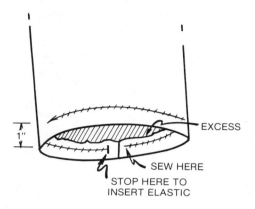

1"

EXCESS

SEW HERE

STOP HERE TO INSERT ELASTIC

Figure 7-13

Pants Length and Completing the Cuffs

The pants are now ready to be cut to final length and fitted with elastic cuffs. Pull the pants on over your usual hiking pants and tie the waist just above the belt-line. Slip two rubber bands over the pants bottoms and slide them up and down to suit you. Walk a few steps, squat, sit, etc., before deciding on a final length. (You may wish to do this in your usual hiking footwear). Mark the bottoms with chalk and remove pants. Measure your ankles at the pants bottoms. Cut two 1/2″ wide soft (underwear) elastic strips 1/2″ larger (i.e., ten per cent smaller, plus 1″ overlap) than your measurement.

Fold both wind pant leg cuffs to be the same length.

Now pin the excess leg fabric to the wrong side. Hem the leg 1″ from the fold line (chalk line), making a sleeve for the elastic in the process (Fig. 7-13). Leave a 2″ gap in this hem seam. Insert one end of the elastic, attached to the threading tool, into this gap and draw the elastic around inside the tube. Check to be certain it has not twisted, then overlap the elastic ends 1″ and stitch several times.

Sew to close the gap in the hem. Try the wind pants on again and test their length standing, sitting, squatting, etc. If everything seems to be okay, trim the cuff seam allowance and carefully heat-seal the fabric.

The wind pants are now complete and may be stuffed into their pocket for a trial. I hope they demonstrate their value and keep you warm on your next trip.

39

Chapter 8
Insulated Booties

When asked why he was pounding his head with a hammer, the small boy replied "because it feels so good when I stop." There is a theory among the uninitiated that this rationale motivates backpackers. I'll have to admit that the luxury of removing my boots after a long day on a rocky trail is hard to equal, and I suppose this lends credence to the theory.

Finding good lightweight footgear to replace those boots around camp, however, is a formidable task. The feet need some small protection when padding around the campsite, lounging, or for that wee hours "call of nature."

The booties in this chapter may fill the bill, in terms of light weight, low cost, warmth, and comfort. They won't suffice for emergency hiking nor as waterproof or mudproof shoes in a wet campsite. But they can keep your feet toasty on a cool evening or before a fire, and even in your sleeping bag, if you dust them off. Besides, we all deserve a bit of luxury and what part of our anatomy deserves it more than those loyal servants that transport us?

Materials

1/3 yard × 44″ uncoated uppers fabric

1/4 yard × 44″ 4 to 7 ounce outsole fabric or leather

8″ × 12″ nylon or cotton rib knit

1/4 yard bonded quilt batting or Polarguard

Making the Pattern

Begin by making a foot outline tracing on newspaper or pattern paper. Place a dot where the ball of your foot behind the big toe hits the traced line. Measure across the tracing from the dot to the widest point to determine the foot width, "A" (see Fig. 8-1a). Now measure the foot length, "B"; then measure the heel width, "C".

The sole pattern consists of two semicircles with radii—

$R = 1/2 A + 3/4″$, and $r = 1/2 C + 3/4″$, connected by two straight lines (Fig. 8-1b). The total length, "L," is equal to the tracing length plus 2-1/4″ ($L = B + 2-1/4″$). Draw it on newspaper or pattern-paper and cut it out. Note: Circular curves can be drawn with a compass or using cups, cans, bowls, etc.

The upper piece pattern is started as shown in Fig. 8-2. Begin by drawing the heel and sole lines at right angles. The heel line, which will be placed along a fold in the pattern paper should be 4-1/4″ long (3-1/4″ for children's sizes). The sole line should be extended to beyond the length of the foot, for the moment (see Fig. 8-2).

Locate the instep point, "X", 4-1/4″ above the sole line at a point 3/4 B (3/4 length of foot) forward of the heel line. Sketch in a curved line connecting the top of the heel line and the instep point "X", with the low point of the curve 1″ below a straight line joining these points (Fig. 8-3).

Place a pencil dot at a point 4″ above the sole line and at distance "B" in front of the heel line; call this point "Y". Draw a straight line from "X" through "Y" and on forward.

Now draw a quarter circle of radius 2R (that is, twice

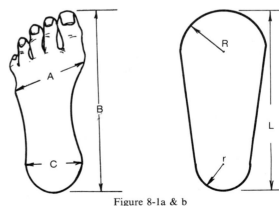

Figure 8-1a & b

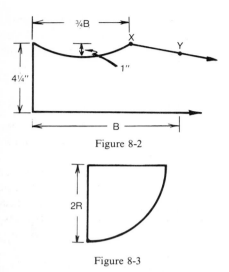

Figure 8-2

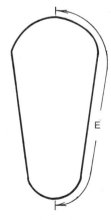

Figure 8-3

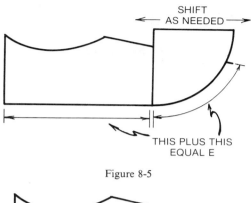

Figure 8-5

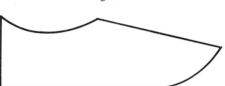

Figure 8-6

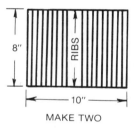

Figure 8-7

the radius of the toe of the sole piece pattern) on a piece of scrap paper and cut it out (Fig. 8-3).

Measure one side of the sole piece pattern edge from center back to center front; call this measurement "E" (Fig. 8-4).

Place the quarter circle cut out on the upper pattern piece and shift it until the sole line plus the quarter circle segment up to the line X-Y are equal to the length "E" (Fig. 8-5).

Use this quarter circle cut-out as a template and draw in the curve required. Now, cut out the uppers pattern piece (Fig. 8-6).

The ankle piece is made of ribbing knit. Fig. 8-7 shows the piece required; no pattern is necessary.

Figure 8-4

Choosing Fabrics

Fabric for the booties uppers should be breathable. Nylon is light in weight and works well, but any woven fabric may be used if the rapid drying properties of synthetic cloth are not required (e.g. for booties used as lounge slippers).

The insole piece should be of breathable fabric, but the outsole should be of coated fabric if you require some measure of moisture resistance. Make the outsole of four to seven-ounce fabric, or even heavier if you want it to last, and place the slick waterproof-coated surface "in" to protect it from abrasion, as well as to provide better traction for the wearer (Fig. 8-8).

If you seek real luxury, you may wish to install leather outsoles, though these will soak through if wet, and weigh a bit more.

The ribbing piece can be of elasticized cotton or synthetic. It is folded during construction to 4" × 10", so if

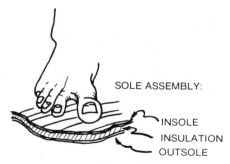

SOLE ASSEMBLY:

INSOLE
INSULATION
OUTSOLE

Figure 8-8

you have some heavy ribbing that need not be doubled, the full 8″ height is not needed. An inexpensive and effective alternative is the ribbing tops from three or four old socks. These may be pieced to provide the two pieces required.

Insulation is best made from *bonded* polyester fiber fill. The bonded fill is sold in many fabric stores in 1″-thick batts in one pound quantities. Be certain it is bonded—a layered batt as for quilt-making—since most stores also carry loose dacron for pillow stuffing. The bonded Fortrel, called Polarguard, is a relatively new product and is not widely available (see Appendix I—Country Ways, Sun Down, Frostline).

Cutting Out

To make one pair of booties you will need two cuff pieces, four uppers pieces, two insole and two outsole pieces. Two uppers and two sole-insulation pieces should be cut to the same patterns, respectively (Fig. 8-9), but 1/4″ smaller all around.

Two uppers pieces can be cut at once with judicious folding of the fabric: the heel line of the uppers pattern piece is placed along a fold, a second fold is made at right angles to the first and the pattern pinned through all layers (Fig. 8-9). Cut out the insulation pieces.

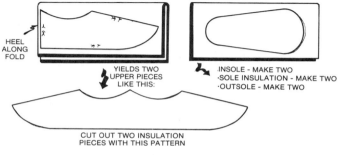

HEEL ALONG FOLD

YIELDS TWO UPPER PIECES LIKE THIS:

·INSOLE - MAKE TWO
·SOLE INSULATION - MAKE TWO
·OUTSOLE - MAKE TWO

CUT OUT TWO INSULATION PIECES WITH THIS PATTERN

Figure 8-9

All uncoated fabric edges should be fused with a match before beginning construction. Since the insulation is already bonded with a resin it is unnecessary to fuse its edges.

Constructing the Booties

Begin construction by sewing two uppers pieces together 1/4″ from their edges, all around, but leave a 2″ gap as shown in Fig. 8-10.

Do *not* turn this uppers sub-assembly inside out. Tuck the insulation piece into the gap you have left and shift it about till it is fully extended (a 12″ ruler or knitting needle may help), then tack it in place at the points shown in Fig. 8-10; triple stitch these 1″ long tack seams. Repeat for the upper of the other bootie.

Repeat these edge-stitching, insulation insertion, and tacking steps for the sole pieces of both booties (Fig. 8-10).

Pin the center of one 10″ edge of ribbing knit fabric to the center top of the wrong side of the uppers assembly (Fig. 8-11). Stretch and pin the ribbing along the uppers edge to the points "X" indicated in Fig. 8-2, leaving a 1/4″ excess unpinned for a front seam allowance. Sew. Fold the ribbing fabric, bringing the other 10″ edge against the right side of the top edge of the uppers assembly. Tuck

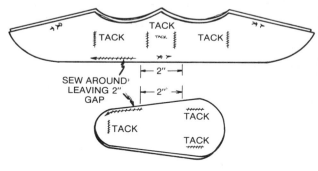

TACK

TACK   TACK   TACK

SEW AROUND LEAVING 2″ GAP

2″

2″

TACK

TACK

TACK

Figure 8-10

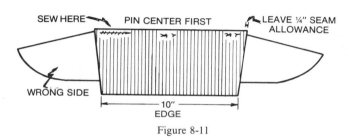

SEW HERE   PIN CENTER FIRST   LEAVE ¼″ SEAM ALLOWANCE

WRONG SIDE

10″ EDGE

Figure 8-11

this 10″ ribbing edge under 1/4″ and pin it in place (Fig. 8-12).

Stitch the ribbing to the uppers assembly close to the tucked edge of the ribbing.

Begin now at the center back of the bottom edge of the uppers assembly and pin it to the center back of the sole, right sides together, such that the raw edges lie on the same side as the raw edges of the ribbing-uppers seam (Fig. 8-13). Pinning the straight edge of the upper to the curve of the heel will make an awkward three-dimensional object to sew, but don't be discouraged. Continue pinning to the toe of the upper, allowing a 1/2″ seam allowance along the edge as you pin, and a 1/2″ excess for the toe to instep seam. Note: If your uppers piece overlaps too much or too little at this point, shift it out or in relative to the sole assembly edge.

Now pin the toe to instep seam and ribbing seam and sew from the toe to the ribbing top leaving a 1/2″ seam allowance (Fig. 8-14). Trim any rough or bumpy seam allowances and re-fuse the fabric edges with heat. Turn the booties right side out and try them on. Now you've got a bit of luxury!

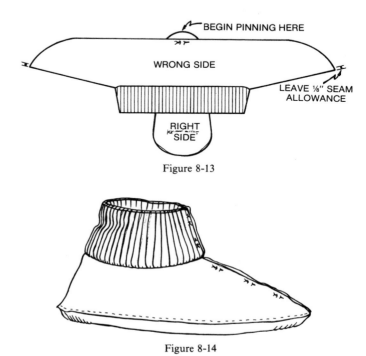

Figure 8-13

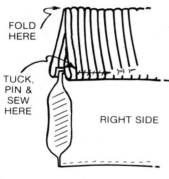

Figure 8-12

Figure 8-14

Chapter 9
Sleeping Bag

If wilderness camping is to be a joy and an experience to be savored, the hiker must plan to rest as well as to travel. Since the labor of backpacking is somewhat greater than most of us encounter in our working lives, the rests must be commensurate. Too many hikers lose the spark after a few hikes because they forget they have come for the renewal (read "rest") as well as the challenge.

Rest requires comfort and some security against the elements. Thin, cold air, sparkling rock and water, and scudding clouds spell beautiful scenery but can create an uncomfortable bedroom.

Down-Filled Nylon—The Industry Standard

The modern, lightweight nylon and down sleeping bag has opened up the wilderness to the backpacker by providing sleeping comfort within reasonable weight limits. He can carry a light, warm retreat on his packframe, a situation that was essentially unavailable fifteen years ago. He has become largely independent of the external environment during adverse weather and at night.

Do you want a down sleeping bag?

Until the last few years there was no real alternative to a down-filled nylon shell sleeping bag if you wanted to backpack. They were the only quality bags on the market light enough to be carried comfortably. Down bags are still considered the ultimate in warmth and lightness, but two new polyester fill materials are successfully competing for a significant share of the backpacker's market. Why is down still so popular, and why are these new fills making inroads? For the answers we must know how a quality sleeping bag is made and tested.

A more complete discussion of sleeping bag design and internal construction is available in most any equipment manufacturer's catalogue. For our purpose, it is necessary to understand only that a sleeping bag is like a double

sack, with fill between the layers and a sleeper inside the inner shell (Fig. 9-1).

The shells are porous to air and to water vapor (perspiration), but prevent the fill from escaping. The fill functions to trap dead air space, discouraging convection of warm air away from the sleeper. A system of baffles, or seams, is used to prevent the fill from shifting and creating "cold spots."

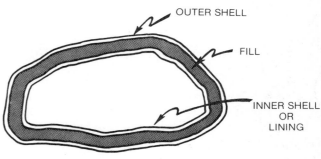

Figure 9-1

Since the hiker's concern in purchasing a sleeping bag is warmth, manufacturers have attempted to provide information by rating their bags. The estimated minimum temperature at which the "average" person would be comfortable in a given sleeping bag is typically called its "rating." A better and more objective measure of a sleeping bag is its loft or thickness—better since it is directly comparable between bags of different manufacturers. Assuming no cold spots—places where the inner and outer shells of a bag are in contact and there is thus no insulation between the sleeper and the cold night—the thicker the bag, the greater the dead air space, and thus the higher the "rating."

Now all of the above discussion assumes that the environment is constant in many ways that it rarely is. Clouds, winds, humidity, altitude, the sleeper's vital parameters, a tent, groundsheet, and sleeping pad all make a world of difference. Please don't throw up your hands in desperation—all further discussion is not useless. A few facts are relevant and even helpful in the choice of a sleeping bag.

First, down, the fine underfeathers of ducks and geese, is measurably superior to all other potential insulators on a warmth-to-weight scale. Modern synthetic insulators such as Dupont Dacron Hollofil II and Celanese Polargard weigh about forty to fifty per cent more, volume for volume.

Nylon is the accepted leader as shell material. It is light, mildew-resistant, and warms up readily. It is also slippery, permitting easy movement within the sleeping bag and can be woven tightly enough to be downproof.

Down and nylon have thus become the industry standard for sleeping bags. They provide the lightest, warmest bags available. They stuff well and thus are not bulky to carry on a pack frame. They are also luxurious, expensive, and a bit extravagant, thus satisfying our urge to have "the finest."

Down

Alternatives to the presently available down bags should be considered by any reasonable hiker. The reasons, especially for one who makes his own equipment, are compelling. Down is fragile: it is eminently "wettable" and when wet it has no loft. It is difficult to dry once wet—an hour or two in a *warm* clothes dryer is required and perhaps days of fire and sunshine in a wilderness setting (if the sun shines). Down is susceptible to mildew when wet and is oxidized when dry by air pollutants, and sunlight speeds this process. A well-cared-for down bag may last many years but will gradually lose its loft and wear out, as does leather, silk, and any other animal product (old down makes great pillow stuffing).

A central controversy among down equipment manufacturers and users these days is whether or not to wash a down bag, to use dry cleaning, or mild soap and water, and how frequently. Anything near a wilderness hiker for eight hours a day, every day, acquires a "scent." The bag shell can be cleaned crudely like an upholstered chair with suds and little water, to avoid wetting the down. But in time this doesn't seem enough.

Dousing in mild soap and water or cleaning fluid (Stoddard's *only*!) gets much dirt out, but does it remove too much natural down oils and promote deterioration? The jury is still out on this question of cleaning.

In an effort to lighten their products, some sleeping bag manufacturers have used nylon mosquito netting for the sewn baffles that maintain the even distribution of fill between the shells. Baffles are necessary and must be installed carefully to be effective; otherwise, the down will leak and cold spots will result. Nylon netting, however, while it is very light, is rather weak and tears easily under the stresses of stuffing and unstuffing and especially soap and water washing (wet down is quite heavy). Better-quality bags now employ somewhat heavier and stronger baffle material. The baffled internal structure of a down bag can make it somewhat more complicated to sew and thus more expensive than a comparably warm synthetic sleeper.

Perhaps the most telling argument against down is its cost. Demand is high and growing and the quality of European goose down available to American makers is said to be falling while the price continues to rise. Retail goose down, in the quality and quantities necessary to make a sleeping bag, is very expensive fill.

If you are determined to have a quality down sleeping bag but are not really wealthy, consider a kit (see Appendix I). At today's prices, the kits are a bargain, but they do require a heavy time commitment for construction.

Synthetic Fill—the Alternative

The price paid by those who choose a synthetic fill sleeping bag is one of weight. Three pounds of fill (Dacron Hollofil II or Polarguard) are required to do the job of two pounds of down in a summer sleeping bag. A winter bag filled with three pounds of down could be replaced by a bag containing approximately four-and-a-half pounds of synthetic fill. Weight is important to a backpacker; sometimes that pound or two is crucial and down must be chosen.

The savings accruing to those who choose synthetic are many and varied. Perhaps the most important savings is in dollars. Bought from a quality manufacturer, a Dacron Hollofil II or Polarguard bag can cost one-third less than a comparably warm down bag. If you make your own, that figure can be cut in half again. I like to think that the extra weight carried by a hiker with a synthetic bag is balanced by the extra weight a down sleeper requires to be protected from wetting. At any rate, a wet synthetic bag is no great problem and when wrung out gently, is warm and almost comfortable—at least one can sleep warm in it. A dousing by rain or creek water will dry in one or two hours with a little sun or wind to help.

This freedom from worry about moisture permits

somewhat greater flexibility for the user of a synthetic fill bag. If the flattest sleeping spot with the best view is exposed to the sky and thus bound to be dewy, he can choose it with impunity: a dew dampened synthetic bag will dry in a few minutes sunshine and any remaining moisture will not damage the fill if it must be stuffed damp. If he has developed the mountain man's ability to ignore foul weather, he can sleep through a mist or short shower with no consequences. In a heavier rain he can simply pull a poncho over his bag (being certain to provide an adequate breathing space) and sleep till morning. This last technique can have dire consequences in a down bag. If the wet weather continues, it can be very difficult to dry down, and body condensation can dampen it as well as rain.

In some applications, synthetic fill is to be chosen despite its greater weight and bulk. Snowshoe hikes, ski touring, winter mountaineering, etc. all subject gear to frequent wetting and cold, damp conditions that discourage drying out. Canoe camping and bicycle tour camping, where weight is somewhat less of a problem than backpacking and moisture a frequent companion, would seem ideal places to employ synthetic fill sleepers.

I feel certain that someday soon man will outdo the goose in the insulation field. Right now synthetic fill is a good competitor in many ways. With respect to the sleeping bag described in this chapter, synthetic fill is chosen primarily because of the ease of construction it makes possible.

The sleeping bag described here has two versions, both of semi-mummy design. The weights are three pounds and four-and-a-half pounds for the "warm-night" and "three-season" bags respectively. They are sized to accommodate an average adult from 5'8" to 6', and the patterns can be easily adjusted to suit larger or smaller sleepers. Both outer and lining shells are nylon—the outer of ripstop, the inner of somewhat less costly aspen cloth taffeta. The bags have a hood. Since the human neck, head, and scalp are the body regions through which the greatest heat loss occurs in a cold environment, an integral hood is required on any effective sleeping bag.

The inner and lining shells are cut from the same pattern, making what's called a non-differential cut. Some manufacturers of fine down bags cut the inner shell of their more expensive models smaller than the outer shell. This is called differential cut and is supposed to prevent cold spots where knees, elbows, and shoulders compress the two shells together. Experts for and against this "thermos bottle" concept are quite heated in their views. With these bags, several considerations mitigate against differential cut construction. First it is more difficult to construct. Second, synthetic fill is less compressible than down and will not shift out of the way under pressure as down will, thus making a differential cut unnecessary. Third, another group of manufacturers say differential cut bags are colder. They suggest that a loose inner shell can fold and conform to the body better and thus eliminate drafts and air spaces the body must heat. For all these reasons, but primarily in the interests of simplicity, the bag we describe is non-differential cut.

The unique feature of this sleeping bag—one that has not yet been tried in a commercial bag—is its tufted construction. The tufts resemble those of a comforter, but in the "three-season" version the shells are separated by polyurethane foam blocks to eliminate cold spots.

Choosing Fabric and Fill

This sleeping bag is intended to compare favorably with the best commercially-produced synthetic fill bags available. If you expect good performance, don't skimp on materials. The place to save is on labor costs, by making your own. The construction will require a good bit of your time and effort, so don't waste your energy on unsatisfactory material.

The shells should be made of nylon of about two ounces per square yard. Ripstop is best for the outer shell, though tightly woven taffeta will serve almost equally well. Taffeta is said to be a bit more abrasion-resistant, while ripstop is less snag-prone. Since down will not be lost from a tear or snag, ripstop is not really essential. The inner shell should be nylon since it (1) "feels" warm after a moment's contact with the skin, (2) is slippery, permitting unimpeded movement during sleep, and (3) does not absorb perspiration and become "clammy" (cotton should be avoided for these three reasons). Taffeta is fine unless you can get a better price on ripstop. Choose a medium color outer for heat retention and a dark inner for its ability to hide dirt.

Nylon is a flammable fabric and thus susceptible to sparks from a campfire and heat and flame from the camp stove. Recent Federal law now demands the use of fire retardant fabric in manufactured tents and sleeping bags, which makes them weigh a bit more but is certainly to be recommended for safety reasons. Still unanswered are questions concerning the health hazards of fabric flame retardants.

If you wish to experiment with the sleeping bag or other insulated gear, a variety of synthetic fills are presently available. Among these are polyurethane foam in sheets or loose chips, unbonded Dacron 88, polyether foam, DuPont Hollofil II (an unbonded but layered loose fiber), Celanese Polarguard batting, and bonded dacron quilt batting. Only the last two of these are suitable as purchased for the sleeping bag project. The first two are available at most fabric stores. The third is used by Ocate, Inc. in making their sleeping bags. It is said to drape well, but I know of no source for obtaining it. DuPont Hollofil II is a wonderfully soft, very compressible fiber but not available in bonded batts. It, therefore, must be bonded by sewing to other cloth. This reduces its loft and increases its weight (available in quilted form from EMS). Polarguard is available at retail prices in two thicknesses—1″ and 1-1/2″. If you intend to use either of these last two materials, Hollofil or Polarguard, see the note below in "cutting out the insulation."

Bonded polyester quilt batting can be purchased in very large sheets in several thicknesses from Sears, Montgomery Ward, J.C. Penney, etc. The best batting I've used was from an upholstery shop: 30″ wide, 1-1/2″ loft, and strongly bonded. The price is low from all sources and, with care in construction, it can be a good insulator and make a fine sleeping bag.

A full-length double slide zipper of 100″ is a good feature to include in your bag. A short, 40″ zipper that opens the bag only to the waist will save a few ounces but cost much in versatility. With a long, across-the-foot zipper the sleeping bag can be opened out flat for quick airing/drying and for use as a comforter for an unexpected house guest. Two full zip bags can be joined as a double sleeper. Finally a full zip bag with a double slide system can be opened at the foot for ventilation on those not-so-cold nights.

Other sewing notions required to complete this project include 6 feet of 3/16″ drawstring cord and two cordlocks. The cord locking devices hold the hood drawstrings much more easily than a knot, and save fumbling in the cold darkness. Two large spools of cotton-wrapped dacron thread are recommended, as the seams are very long. Buy thread to match the outer shell.

This is the time to get out the card table mentioned in the chapter on tools. The sleeping bag is a large, bulky, and sometimes exasperating thing to sew, and supporting it on a card table can relieve a bit of the frustration. The drawstring threading tool will be needed for the hood. The tufting and sewing of the fill will require about half a skein (2 oz.) of two-ply sport weight synthetic knitting yarn and a sharp-pointed, #2 crewel hand needle. Also required for the "three-season" version are the foam blocks for the tufts. They can be cut from 1″ or 2″-thick

sheet polyurethane foam. Four square feet should be sufficient.

Once these materials and tools have been assembled, you can commence construction by making the patterns.

Materials

Outer shell fabric: 4-2/3 yards ripstop nylon

Inner shell fabric: 4-2/3 yards taffeta or ripstop nylon

Nylon #5 or #7 chain-type, 100″ zipper

Nine feet of 1/8″ sash cord

Two cord locking devices

Nine feet of 2″ wide nylon belt stiffening

#18 or #20 chenille needlework hand needle

One 2 ounce skein 4-ply knitting yarn (color to match outer shell fabric)

Note: For the "three-season" version, also needed are: 4 square feet of 1″-thick polyurethane foam or 2 square feet of 2″-thick foam

Tools

soldering iron

card table

chalk, marking pen

Fill

"WARM-NIGHT" VERSION

Four yards of 30″ wide, 1-1/2″ thick bonded dacron quilt batting (upholstery shop) or

Four yards of 8 ounce per yard 30-44″ wide Celanese Polarguard or

One or two 66″ × 90″ bonded polyester quilt batts to equal 1-1/4″ to 1-3/4″ total loft (Sears, J. C. Penney, Montgomery Ward)

"THREE-SEASON" VERSION

Eight yards of 30″ wide × 1-1/2″ thick bonded dacron batting, or

Seven to eight yards of 8 to 10-ounce per yard 32-44″ Polarguard (length needed depends on width), or Hollofil/Ripstop Quilted Composite from EMS

Two 66″ × 90″ quilt batts to equal 2-1/4″ to 3″ total loft

A Word About Size

The bag dimensions given in Fig. 9-2 are suitable for a person about 5′8″ to 6′ in height. For a larger or smaller adult, adjust the hip to foot length of the bag but change no other dimensions. For a person 5′1″ or less, it may be necessary to reduce the hip to shoulder circumference as well as shorten the length. If possible, try a sleeping bag belonging to a friend, and use its dimensions to guide your pattern making.

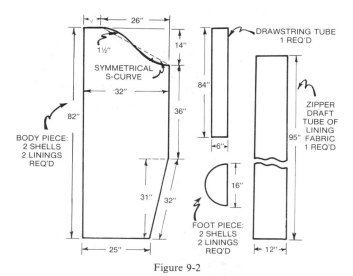

Figure 9-2

Making the Patterns (Both Versions)

The shapes and dimensions of inner lining, outer shell, and fill pieces are identical and symmetric right and left hand. Therefore, only one pattern piece is required for these pieces. The foot pieces are similar and can also be cut out using just one pattern piece. Both pieces are shown with dimensions in Fig. 9-2. The zipper flap piece and drawstring sleeve are simple rectangles and can be drawn directly on the fabric used to make them. Patterns can be drawn on newspaper, newsprint, pattern paper, muslin, or drawn directly on the nylon fabric with chalk.

Cutting Out (Both Versions)

Cut all fabric pieces from the fabrics you have chosen. Note that the drawstring tube and zipper baffle can be pieced together from scraps of shell and lining fabric, respectively. Since the fabric raw edges are so long, it is recommended that you set up the soldering iron fusing gadget (described in Chapter 2) to seal the edges against

raveling. Because the fill material is bonded, edge-fusing is unnecessary.

Sewing the Shells (Both Versions)

The bag is constructed in sub-assemblies; the outer shell with its accessories, the inner shell, and the fill. These sub-assemblies are then joined to complete the bag. It is important to keep in mind that the wrong sides of the outer shell and lining are to be in contact with the fill. Their seam allowances must be sewn to lie against the fill.

The first construction step is to assemble the outer shell. Align, pin, and stitch right and left hand shell pieces right sides together along centerline, using a 5/8″ seam allowance (Fig. 9-3). Fold, pin, and fell-stitch seam allowance 1/4″ from centerline. To fell this seam, it is easiest to fold up the excess fabric that must pass under the sewing arm and clip it with clothespins. Beginning at this centerline seam, align and pin 1/2″ from the raw edges the curved edge of one shell footpiece with the foot edge of the shell body (Fig. 9-4). Be certain the seam allowances are on the same side as those of the centerline seam. With the foot piece on top, stitch along the pin line adjusting the raw edge alignment as you proceed. Repeat for the other shell foot piece. Fold, pin, and fell-stitch the seam allowances toward the shell body.

Repeat these steps to complete the lining centerline and foot piece seams. The last step in preparing the fabric shells for the accessory pieces is to fold and hem-stitch all

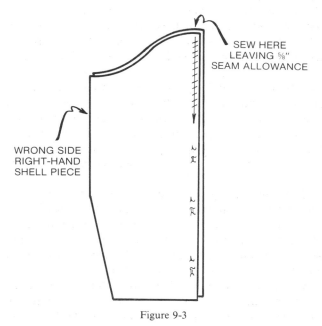

Figure 9-3

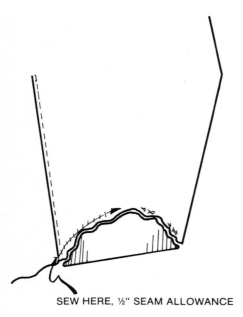

SEW HERE, ½" SEAM ALLOWANCE

Figure 9-4

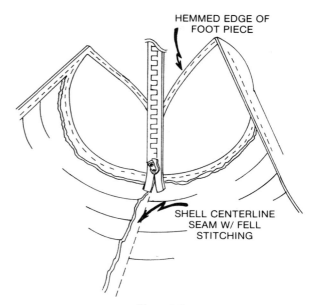

VIEW OF INSIDE OF SHELL FOOT
WITH ZIPPER IN PLACE

HEMMED EDGE OF
FOOT PIECE

SHELL CENTERLINE
SEAM W/ FELL
STITCHING

Figure 9-5

remaining raw edges (hood-, zipper- and foot-edges of both outer shell and lining 1/4" toward the wrong side). Pinning should not be necessary.

Installing the Zipper

The zipper tapes are now sewn to the shell zipper edges. Zip the zipper closed and pin its lower end (the end with the slides and socket) about 1" below the hemmed edges of the foot pieces and along the centerline seam allowances. Be certain the pull tab faces outward (if there's only one) and the zipper tapes lie on the wrong side of the shell (Fig. 9-5).

Pin the left hand zipper tape (shown) to the corresponding hemmed shell edge. Allow 1/8" between the zipper teeth and the hemmed fabric edge. Stop pinning just above the foot piece-body piece seam. Bring the left foot piece up to the zipper, align the seams across the zipper, and pin the left hand foot piece edge to the left zipper tape (Fig. 9-6).

Continue pinning up the hood edge of both shell halves, alternately zipping to check alignment and unzipping to pin. The hood edges should match to within about 1/2". You will end up with several inches of excess zipper which should be shortened and cut off as described in the "Techniques" section of Chapter 2.

When you have checked that the zipper slide will not catch the surrounding fabric and are satisfied with the alignment, sew the zipper to the outer shell 1/8" from the

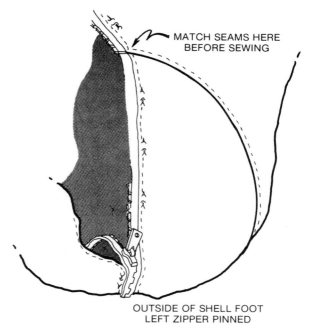

MATCH SEAMS HERE
BEFORE SEWING

OUTSIDE OF SHELL FOOT
LEFT ZIPPER PINNED

Figure 9-6

hemmed fabric edge (i.e., 1/4" from the zipper teeth). Do not bother to double stitch these seams as later sewing will reinforce them.

Adding the Hood Drawstring Sleeve
(Both Versions)

The hood's function as a trap for body warmth, especially that lost by the head and neck, is enhanced by the adjustable drawstring closure. The drawstring is enclosed by the double-thick sleeve described here.

Either outer or lining fabric may be chosen for use in making the drawstring sleeve. Cut the piece to the dimensions shown in Fig. 9-2. Fold the piece along its length and stitch 1/4″ from the raw edges down the long side and across one end. Invert the resulting tube over a yardstick or dowel. Fold the raw "end" edges in 1/4″ and topstitch all around the piece close to this edge and the seamed edges (Fig. 9-7).

Fold the piece along its length (Fig. 9-7) and align the long top-stitched edges with the right side of the hemmed shell hood edge and pin (Fig. 9-8). Machine baste the drawstring tube in place 1/4″ from the aligned edges.

Again, do not reflex or double-stitch this seam, as it will be reinforced with later stitching.

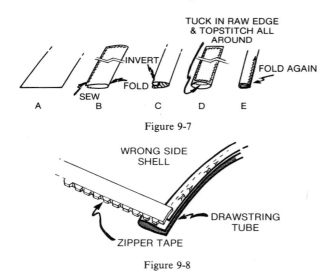

Figure 9-7

Figure 9-8

Making and Attaching the Insulated
Zipper Flap (Both Versions)

Even the tightest of zippers is no barrier to wind penetration. The zipper and its adjacent seams constitute a significant chink in the backpacker's armor against the cold. This gap is best filled with an insulated draft tube, backing the zipper on the lining side. The zipper draft tube should be cut from inner shell fabric or it may be pieced together from scraps (see Fig. 9-2 for dimensions).

To protect the draft tube from catching in the zipper, a backing piece of 2″ belt stiffener is sewn to the wrong side of the surface that will face the zipper.

Fold the zipper draft tube piece longitudinally right sides together, position the belt stiffener against the wrong side, centered between the fold and one long raw edge (see Fig. 9-9a); pin. Unfold the draft tube fabric and sew the belt stiffener piece in place 1/4″ from its edges all around (Fig. 9-9b). Fold the zipper draft tube again longitudinally right sides together, belt stiffener to the outside. Sew across one short edge and down the length of the aligned long edges with a 1/4″ seam allowance. Invert this tube over a yardstick or broom handle and carefully clip the end stitching to form an open-ended tube (see Fig. 9-9c). Topstitch close to the long seam.

Align the topstitched seam of the zipper flap tube with the right side of the left hand edge of the lining piece (Fig. 9-10) from the hood edge to the body centerline seam. The belt stiffener side of the tube must face up so the unstiffened side of the draft tube is in contact with the lining.

Pin the tube in place and cut away any excess length, leaving about 1/2″ extra length as a seam allowance at each end. Stitch the zipper tube 1/4″ from the aligned long edges. Do not fill the tube or close its ends yet.

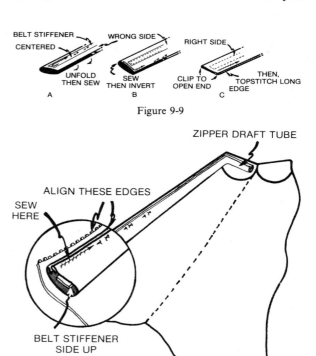

Figure 9-9

Figure 9-10

Cutting Out the Insulation (Both Versions)

Using the patterns made for the shell and foot pieces, cut out one or two batting pieces, depending on choice of materials and design. These should be full width (60″) and length (80″) and require no center-line seam if you choose polyester quilt batting as insulation. If you have purchased 44″-wide Celanese Polarguard or other narrow fill, it will be necessary to abut the midseam edges and *loosely* overhand stitch the right hand and left hand sides together. Do this for both layers of insulation if you are making the "three-season" (see Fig. 9-11). Save all scrap insulation for extra layers in the chest-to-hip areas or for other projects.

(Note: Some fill is bonded with a water-soluble resin that gradually disappears with repeated washings. Inquire about this when buying. Dacron Hollofil II is an unbonded fill. With either of these materials it is necessary to use the following procedure. Make two nylon mosquito netting pieces the shape of the sleeping bag body but about 12″ longer. Layer the fill evenly between these cloth pieces and pin and baste with five or six passes widthwise on the sewing machine. Some loft will be lost, but this will prevent shifting of the insulation and resulting cold spots. Fluffing between seams will minimize the loss of loft.)

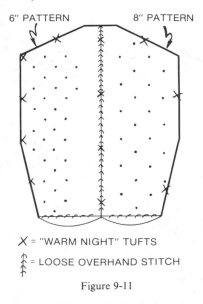

6″ PATTERN   8″ PATTERN

X = "WARM NIGHT" TUFTS

= LOOSE OVERHAND STITCH

Figure 9-11

Stabilizing the Fill (Both Versions)

The whole purpose of a sleeping bag is to trap still air in a layer around a warm body—yours—to retard heat loss to the colder environment. Both versions of this bag were

constructed using tufts to hold the batts in place, a method well-suited to the materials from which it is intended to be made. Sewing (quilting) is unnecessary with a layered batt fill like bonded polyester. Sewing also creates seam line "cold spots" through which warmth escapes. Tufts eliminate most of this problem by reducing the areas of contact between outer and inner shells (cold spots) to single points rather than lines. My goal in making the "three-season" bag was to reduce these cold spots altogether by tufting through thick foam blocks. An additional benefit derived from foam block tufts is an increased distance between shells: the foam blocks chosen—about 2″ high by 1″ square—act as pillars separating the fill layers.

The resulting air space between the fill layers is not all "dead"; convection currents can form and carry some heat away, unless further insulation is added. But the amount of additional insulation is small, and, since none of the insulation used must bear the weight of the shell, it can attain greater loft than without the foam tufts.

There are disadvantages to foam pillar tufts, too. They make the bag a bit bulkier and more difficult to stuff as well as increasing the difficulty of construction somewhat. But I feel that the benefits outweigh the disadvantages.

The "warm night" bag construction requires no foam blocks. The assembly details parallel those given below for the "three-season" version, but tufting is needed only in the locations shown in Figure 9-11.

The following details describe the internal construction of the prototype "three-season" bag, and you may follow them verbatim if you wish. I am quite pleased with this bag and am sure it would also serve you well. However, if you prefer to experiment with a slightly different technique, be my guest.

The first step is to make a "sandwich": shell, right-side-down; batting layer number "1", batting layer number "2", and lining, right-side-up (Fig. 9-12).

Align everything as well as possible, ignoring the foot pieces. Pins won't work well in the thick stuff, so don't bother. Begin to tuft immediately about 6″ from the foot end along the midline seam by drawing that long sharp needle (chenille #18 or #20) threaded with 2-ply synthetic knitting worsted yarn through the lining and fill batt "2" (Fig. 9-12). Push the needle through (use a thimble) a 1-1/2″ cube of polyurethane foam, then continue through batt "1" and shell layers at the centerline seam. Turn the needle over and push it back through all layers, emerging no more than 1/4″ from where it entered. Draw the yarn snug but not tight, permitting maximum loft. Tie a square knot and an extra overhand knot and clip the yarn ends to 1-1/2″.

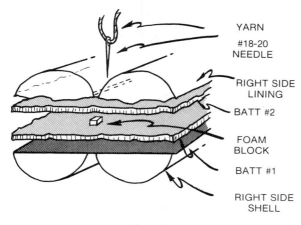

YARN

#18-20 NEEDLE

RIGHT SIDE LINING

BATT #2

FOAM BLOCK

BATT #1

RIGHT SIDE SHELL

Figure 9-12

Repeat this tufting step about 6″ from the head end of the midline seam and at two equidistant points between (Fig. 9-11). The layers are now fixed and the assembly may be moved, rolled up, or folded, until the next tufting session.

I chose to use the scrap batting pieces to form a third layer beneath my hips and shoulders. With three layers of batting in the area of the back, hips, and shoulders, I felt no need of foam blocks to add further loft (they also tend to make sensible bumps under the sleeper).

For this reason, I left the blocks out in this area.

The sides and top of the "three-season" bag should be tufted using 2″ thick blocks (1″ or 1-1/2″ square). The tufts should be placed in a diamond pattern and spaced at 6″ to 10″ apart—depending on your patience (Fig. 9-11). Be sure to work out from midline to sides. A fabric or paper grid with holes spaced at the desired intervals is a valuable tool. Marking carefully on both shells in chalk will pay off in wrinkle-free tuft alignment.

I urge you *not* to cut off the tuft yarn immediately at the knot. Synthetic yarn, while more wear resistant than natural fibers is also more prone to unknotting itself in time. The 1-1/2″ tails will not interfere with your use of the bag and will permit you to tighten and retie tufts if needed.

Tuft to within about 6″ of the shell zipper edges before beginning on the foot area. Position the foot insulation pieces and hand-sew them to the body insulation pieces with the crewel needle and knitting yarn. Use a loose overhand stitch. Tuft each foot section in four or five places.

The two bonded polyester layers used in this construction can be made considerably warmer by filling the intervening air spaces with dacron fill scraps. The foam pillars and fibrous roof and floor in these spaces seem to

"hold on" to these scraps well, and mine have needed no further stabilization. I slid narrow strips of fill lengthwise between the foam pieces in the upper bag and put none around the legs.

Closing the Shells

Pin the edge of the right hand lining foot piece in place 1/8″ from the zipper teeth. Continue pinning, checking to see that shell and lining foot-body seams align. The hood edges should also align within 1/2″. Zip the zipper to check for snags, then sew along the pin line. One or two card tables can help support the bulk of the bag during the work on these long awkward seams.

The left lining edge bears the zipper insulation tube. Pin this edge to the zipper tape and shell as described above (Fig. 9-13).

Again check foot-body seam and hood-edge alignment of shell and lining and zip the zipper to be certain it doesn't catch the fabric. Sew the shells together along the pin line. Relax and admire your work; that was a tough one.

Crawl in the bag and find the deepest comfortable spot. Mark the place where the top of your head meets the bag midline. Now is the time for final adjustment of length; there should be an additional 10″ in length beyond the point marked. If the bag exceeds this length and you are not planning to grow longer, remove the hood drawstring sleeve and cut off the excess length to save weight; re-hem the edges and re-sew the tube in place.

Fold the drawstring sleeve out and pin the inner shell hood edge in place, aligned with the outer shell hood edge (Fig. 9-14).

The zipper draft tube can now be filled with scraps of

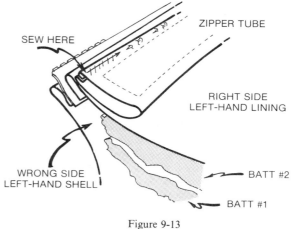

SEW HERE

ZIPPER TUBE

RIGHT SIDE LEFT-HAND LINING

WRONG SIDE LEFT-HAND SHELL

BATT #2

BATT #1

Figure 9-13

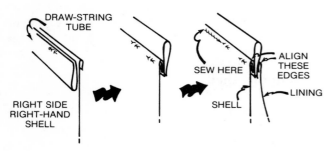

Figure 9-14

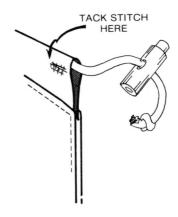

Figure 9-15

fill. Don't stuff it so full that it becomes rigid. Use a yardstick and work from both ends. A strong light source may help you find gaps in the fill. Tuck in the seam allowances at the tube ends about 1/2", and topstitch to close. The tube should be loosely tacked to the zipper tape at about five places along its length to bring it under the zipper when closed.

Insert a 1/4" "parachute cord" drawstring using the drawstring tool. Center the cord and stitch over the cord through the drawstring sleeve at the centerline seam. Stitch close to the cord where it exits the ends of the sleeve (Fig. 9-15) leaving only enough room for the cord to slide through easily. Slip a cord lock onto each end of the cord and tie a "figure 8" knot (see Fig. 2-5, Chapter 2) close to the heat-fused end.

That completes the sleeping bag. Crawl in and try it out. I hope you enjoy it. The "warm night" version will fit nicely in the sleeping bag compartment of the soft pack. The "three-season" version needs a stuff sack about 10" diameter by 20" long. The next chapter tells you how to make your own.

Chapter 10
The Stuff Sack

Down and synthetic insulated equipment items are bulky and would be difficult to carry were it not for stuff sacks. These invaluable containers make possible compression of sleeping bags, jackets, and other fluffy wilderness gear into smaller, more manageable, and less easily-damaged packages.

Two designs are described in this chapter: square bottom and round bottom. Dimensions are given for sacks to contain the two sleeping bags described in Chapter 9 and the vest/jacket in Chapter 13.

With only slight modification, stuff sacks of any required size can be made with these designs.

Materials

Note: The following is suitable for making a stuff sack (11″ diameter × 19″) suitable for a "three-season" sleeping bag

1-1/8 yards coated nylon, 4 ounces per yard

1-1/3 yards × 3/16″ nylon lace

1 cordlock (optional)

Stuff sacks are inevitably in short supply, it seems, and the wise equipment maker should consider making extras. Most pack items become more convenient and accessible when kept in a stuff sack. Some other examples of "stuff-able" gear: tent and poles, cook kit with stove, first aid supplies, dry clothes and underwear, camera equipment, dirty clothes, fishing gear, (dirty) groundsheet or sleepingbag cover, and food stock supply.

Choosing a Fabric

A top quality sleeping bag stuff sack is a thing of beauty. It must be sturdy as it receives considerable stress, abrasive wear, and even attacks by fauna and flora. How does one choose a fabric to meet these needs? Some equipment makers have, in the past, argued that uncoated fabric stuff bags, because they can "breathe," permit some drying of a moist sleeping bag while hiking, and thus are to be preferred. Most have now conceded that this benefit is small compared to the risk of wetting by rain or during a stream crossing. While even a coated stuff sack will leak at its seams and mouth, the protection it provides from moderate rain and accidental dunking speak in its favor.

Tough, durable, waterproof fabrics are available from many backpacking equipment suppliers (see Appendix III). Tightly-woven nylon coated with polyvinyl seems to be well suited to stuff sack needs, and weights of four to eight ounces per square yard are needed to withstand the strain of stuffing a sleeping bag. Coated Dacron, which is now becoming available for backpacking uses, should be superior in this application, since its lack of stretch prevents the loosening of stitching and cracking of waterproof coatings.

Figures 10-1 R and S show the pieces to be cut for construction of round-bottom and square-bottom stuff sacks, respectively. Dimensions to be used for making

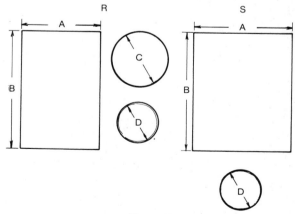

Figure 10-1

stuff sacks of both designs for both the "three-season" and "warm-night" sleeping bags and the insulated jacket in Chapter 13 are given in the accompanying table:

Dimensions in Inches

	ROUND BOTTOM				SQUARE BOTTOM			
	A	B	C	D	A	B	D	E
Three-Season	21-1/2	36-1/2	13	7-1/2	28	38-1/2	7-1/2	6
Warm-Night	19	27	9-1/2	6	24	29	6	5
Insulated Jacket	14	22	8	—	17	24	—	4

The dimensions given are determined as follows: Bottom disc 11″ plus 1″ seam allowance all round = 13″ diameter disc. Body: length = 19″ plus 1″ at bottom, 1-1/2″ at top for drawstring tube = 21-1/2″; circumference: $c = \pi D = 3.14 \times 11'' = 34.5''$ plus 1″ at each edge for seam allowances, that is, 36.5″. Dust cover 7.5″ diameter (approximately two-thirds the finished diameter of bag).

Construction of the Stuff Sack (Both Round Bottom and Square Bottom Versions)

Before starting to sew, mark a seam line 1″ from the raw edge on the wrong (coated) side of the bottom disc for round bottom version. Mark a seam line on the bottom of the body, for both versions, 1″ from the raw edge with a marking pen (it will not be visible when the bag is completed). Note: The coated side is used for the inside (wrong side) of the stuff sack because normal wear and tear would abrade the waterproof coating and render it useless.

Set your sewing machine for not less than ten stitches to the inch. Begin construction by folding back 1″ of the upper corners of the short edges of the body piece, fold toward the wrong side as shown in Fig. 10-2, and taper the fold to disappear 4″ below the upper edge. Sew 1/8″ from the folded edge. Trim seam allowance to 1/4″ beyond seam, if you wish.

Next fold the upper long edge of the body piece 1/2″ down the wrong side and stitch 1/8″ from the raw edge (Fig. 10-2).

Now fold this fold under 1″, to the wrong side, pin and stitch in place with two rows of stitching spaced at 1/8″ (Fig. 10-3). You have just completed the drawstring tube.

Now sew the body tube right sides together along its length 1″ from the aligned "A" edges (Fig. 10-4). Stop about 3″ short of the drawstring tube top. Fold the seam allowances down, both to one side, and stitch them in place with two rows of stitching, holding the fabric firmly to prevent puckering (Fig. 10-5). Again, stop below the drawstring tube.

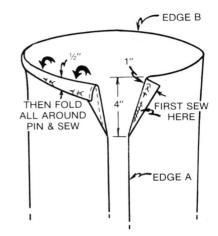

Figure 10-2

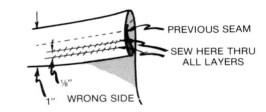

Figure 10-3

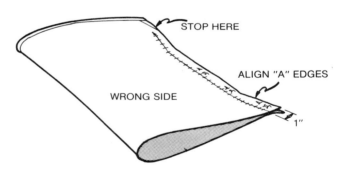

Figure 10-4

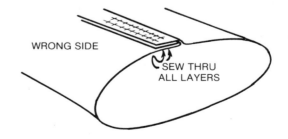

Figure 10-5

Attaching the Bottom Disc (Round Bottom Version Only)

The next seam can be difficult unless you take time to pin carefully. Begin placing the bottom disc against the bottom edge of the body cylinder right sides together so that the marking pen lines align. Continue aligning and pinning along the seam line all around. You may very well end up with a bit of excess fabric on either piece; don't get mad: theory and practice don't always mesh perfectly. If there is "too much" bottom disc, go around and shift the pins so that the bottom disc edge overlaps the body piece; vice versa if there's too much side (Fig. 10-6).

When the pins make a satisfactory circle so that there's no excess in either piece, sew the seam *twice* around with the second stitching line just outside the first (that is, a bit closer to the raw edges).

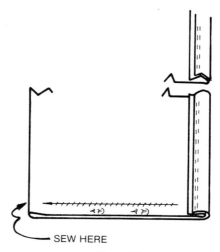

Figure 10-7

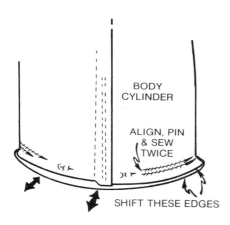

Figure 10-6

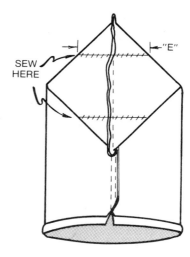

Figure 10-8

Completing the Square Bottom (Square Bottom Version Only)

Pin and sew across the lower ("B") edge from the "A" edge seam to the fold (Fig. 10-7). Fold the stuff sack bottom as shown in Fig. 10-8. Carefully align the bottom ("B") seam with the "A" seam and sew across corner. Refold, aligning "B" seam with fold opposite "A" seam, and sew across corner. Position these seams so that their length is as given in column "E" in the table of dimensions.

Note: When designing your own square bottom stuff sacks, the greatest volume is obtained when the seams "E" are separated by a distance, E, along the "B" seam.

The Dust Flap (Required only on Stuff Sacks Carried Outside the Pack)

The dust flap disc is now sewn in place with its right side against the wrong side of the body seam and drawstring closure area as pictured in Fig. 10-9.

A 1/4" nylon or cotton lace or cord may now be inserted into the drawstring tube, using either the tool described in Chapter 2 or a large safety pin as a "needle." Stretch the bag mouth, pull the cord taut, and cut off the excess, leaving 6" tails on both ends. Fuse the cord ends if necessary and add a drawstring clamp if you wish. Otherwise, tie a "figure eight" or other large knot (see Fig. 2-5, Chapter 2) in each end of the cord. *Stitch* and

61

backstitch the cord in place at the point opposite the openings. This will prevent you from "losing" one end of the cord in the tube some dark cold morning, but will not hinder the functioning of the drawstring.

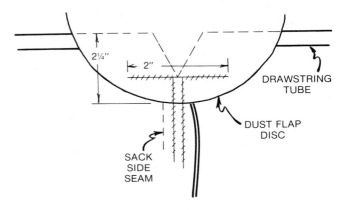

Figure 10-9

Chapter 11
Gaiters, Low and High

Gaiters are the hiker's equivalent of spats or puttees. They function to protect the lower legs and keep snow and/or pebbles out of the boots. Mountaineers are consistent users of high gaiters. These are most useful when traversing deep snow, either while hiking or on skis. Low gaiters are the favorites of nordic or cross-country skiers on prepared trails and hikers who scramble across steep scree or frequent dusty or sandy places.

Most trail hikers have probably encountered conditions where gaiters would be desirable. Not all hiking areas or trails warrant their use, however, so be judicious when deciding to carry their weight. Sewing up a pair can readily be accomplished in an afternoon. Also they are an excellent gift for most any hiker and quite inexpensive. An ardent equipment maker can almost always justify making up a new "toy" by comparing the cost of making things with buying them. If you have not yet thought up a reason to try making the gaiters, low or high, described in this chapter, well, maybe you have superior sales resistance.

Materials

Note: Dimensions for low gaiters given in parentheses

One yard (1/2 yard) coated or water repellent outer fabric

One yard (1/2 yard) uncoated lining such as nylon taffeta or ripstop (optional)

Two yards (1-1/2 yards) 3/4" or 5/8" stiff elastic

Four (0) eyelets (optional)

1-1/3 yard of 3/16" nylon lace

Two 16" (Two 7", optional) separating zippers

Four (3) snap sets or Velcro "dot" sets

Four (4) 1/4" grommets

Two (2) large hooks (from Dritz hook and eye set)

Should you consider waterproof gaiters? Waterproof gaiters, if snug fitting, will keep your socks fairly dry if your foot dips into the water of a creek or bog crossing, and will keep liquid rain out for hours. A weight-bearing step in water above your boot-top will soak your foot, gaiters or not. With waterproof fabric, however, the natural ventilation of boots as you step, pumping air in and out, is prevented. Waterproof gaiters, then, lead to an accumulation of perspiration in the boots, and with high gaiters, in the calf area. Water-repellent, breathable gaiters have no such perspiration problems and are thus more comfortable, provided they are not soaked through from outside moisture sources. Dewy meadow grass, rain-soaked brush along trails, deep, wet spring snow, and rain can soon defeat the moisture protection provided by water-repellent gaiters. The choice between waterproof and water-repellent gaiters finally depends on the areas you hike and the weather you usually encounter.

Choosing Fabric for the Gaiters

Waterproof gaiters are best made of coated nylon fabric of 6 to 10 ounces per square yard. They will take much scraping and scratching from rock and snow and brush and will be heavy enough to survive it. They need not be lined unless you wish to depend on them for warmth; and if this is the case, consider mountaineer's overboots or eskimo mukluks, as they may better suit your needs.

Top quality, water-repellent, breathable gaiters are made of nylon and cotton 60-40 cloth or a similar Dacron and cotton tightly-woven blend, and are lined with ripstop or nylon taffeta for an extra measure of repellency. Choose a color that won't offend your eye when dirty, because washing with soap removes some of the repellent quality of the cloth.

Making a Pattern and Cutting Out

Make a pattern from newspaper or pattern paper using Fig. 11-1, if you want high gaiters, or Fig. 11-2 for low gaiters. A pattern is really needed only if you intend to make more than one pair of gaiters; otherwise, the dimensions can be sketched directly on the outer fabric. If you plan to line the gaiters, fold the lining fabric and place it inside the folded outer material (Fig. 11-3). One cut around the pattern lines will then yield all four required pieces: two outers and two linings. Using the same technique, cut two zipper flap outers and liners. Heat fuse all uncoated synthetic fabric edges.

Note: All subsequent sections are designated for "high" or "low" gaiters. Ignore those parts not pertinent to your project.

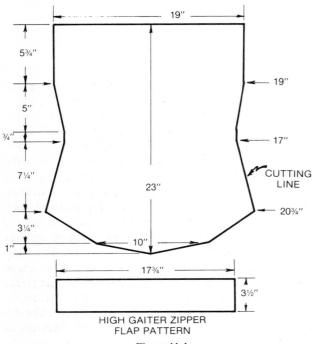

HIGH GAITER PATTERN

HIGH GAITER ZIPPER FLAP PATTERN

Figure 11-1

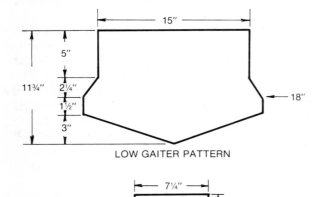

LOW GAITER PATTERN

LOW GAITER FLAP (OPTIONAL SEE TEXT)

Figure 11-2

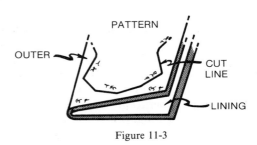

Figure 11-3

To Line or Not to Line (High and Low Gaiters)

If you choose to line a water-repellent outer fabric for extra warmth and repellency, pin the outer and liner pieces, right sides together, and sew 5/8" from the edges all around, leaving a 3" gap unsewn (Fig. 11-4a). Invert the assembly, that is, tuck the liner and the outer through the unsewn gap. This places the raw seam edges inside and the right sides of the fabric pieces out. Use a knitting needle or other rod to poke out the corners and sharpen the angles, then topstitch around the perimeter 1/8" from the edges, closing the gap in the process.

If you are making unlined gaiters, fold all fabric edges

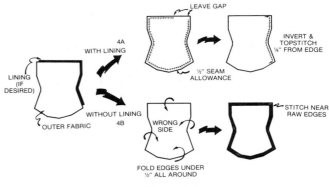

Figure 11-4

5/8″ toward the wrong side (slick side if you are using coated fabric), and stitch close to the raw edge (Fig. 11-4b).

Installing the Ankle Elastic (High Gaiters)

The first step in constructing the high gaiters is to install the ankle elastic in the narrow area of the gaiter body. Choose 5/8″ or 3/4″ wide stiff elastic for this application (Soft "underwear" elastic is too weak to make these stout fabrics crinkle properly.) Adjust the sewing machine to about five stitches per inch and put the presser foot down hard. Use chalk and a straight edge to mark two lines on the lining side as guides (Fig. 11-5). Cut a 12″ length of elastic and pin its ends so that they align with the fabric edges. Place the assembly under the sewing head, lower the presser foot, and stretch the elastic between the chalk lines. Keep this tension while you sew 1/4″ from the elastic edge. Stretch again as you sew 1/4″ from the other edge of the elastic. Admire your crinkly ankle elastic, then repeat these steps for the other gaiter body.

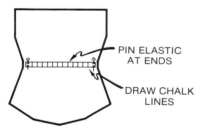

PIN ELASTIC AT ENDS

DRAW CHALK LINES

Figure 11-5

Installing the Instep Elastic (High and Low Gaiters)

The upper and instep elastic bands are encased in tubes formed by folding the upper and lower gaiter edges toward the wrong side and sewing them in place. The folds should be 1″ (Fig. 11-6) and the stitching close to the fabric edge.

Sew the lower elastic band tube first. Its shape is complicated by the angles in the lower edge: the solution lies in folding and pinning a "wrinkle" at each angle as shown in Fig. 11-6. Insert a stiff or soft elastic strip 5/8″ or 3/4″ wide and 16″ long (high gaiters) or 14″ long (low gaiters) and sew it in place at the ends of the tube only.

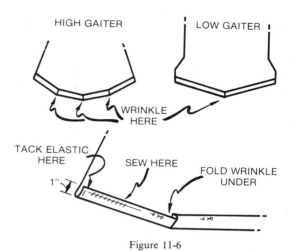

HIGH GAITER   LOW GAITER

WRINKLE HERE

TACK ELASTIC HERE

SEW HERE

FOLD WRINKLE UNDER

1″

Figure 11-6

Installing the Upper Elastic (High and Low Gaiters)

A 12″ length (high gaiters) or 10″ length (low gaiters) of 5/8″ or 3/4″ wide elastic can be installed in a sleeve made by folding the upper edge of the body assembly 1″ toward the wrong side. Sew the ends of the elastic in place at the ends of the sleeve (Fig. 11-7).

A more comfortable and neater upper elastic can be made for the high gaiters by using drawstrings and elastic in combination: Place two 3/16″ eyelets 1-1/2″ below the topstitched upper edge of the body assembly (see Fig. 11-8), centered and 3/4″ apart, so that the smooth side of each eyelet faces the front outside of the gaiter. Fold the gaiter assembly 1″ toward the wrong side and sew in place over the topstitching (Fig. 11-7).

Next make up two elastic lace drawstring assemblies, as shown in Fig. 11-9. Stitch a 4″ piece of 3/4″ wide stiff elastic to a 12″ piece of 1/8″ or 3-1/6″ wide flat nylon lace. (Note: Be sure to heat-fuse the lace ends.)

Thread each lace end through the sleeve and out the nearer eyelet. Stitch the elastic ends securely in place through all layers at the end of the sleeves. The lace can now be tied snug over bare legs or baggy pants with equal facility.

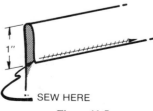

1″

SEW HERE

Figure 11-7

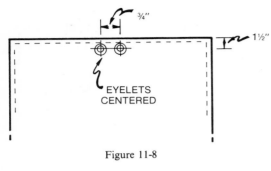

Figure 11-8

Figure 11-9

Installing the Zipper (High and Low Gaiters)

The high gaiters require two 16″ separating zippers, size 5, preferably nylon ones to discourage freezing up. The low gaiters use two 7″ separating zippers. The only source I have found for the 7″ separating zippers is by special order from EMS. A better alternative for the do-it-yourselfer is to purchase the shortest (non-Coil) separating zipper and shorten it by the method described in the "Techniques" section of Chapter 2. The 16″ size zipper for the high gaiter is more widely available.

A snap closure, in lieu of a zipper, works well for the low gaiters. Three or four snaps installed on the optional "zipper" flap could substitute nicely for a zipper in most applications. High gaiters demand a zipper closure. The snap system would leave too many large gaps.

If you do decide to use a zippered closure on the low gaiters, you may, as you choose, install or leave off the zipper flap piece.

Separate the two zipper halves. Pin them to the lining (wrong) sides of the zipper (vertical) edges of the gaiter assembly, being certain that the slide starter is at the bottom and the pull tab faces the right side of the fabric (see Fig. 11-10). Assure adequate clearance for the zipper slide. Fix a zipper foot to your machine and with a single seam sew each zipper tape in place about 1/8″ from the gaiter edge (over the topstitching).

The Zipper Flap Construction and Installation (High and Low Gaiters)

A zipper flap is recommended for protection of the long

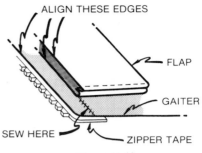

Figure 11-10

zipper on the high gaiters. It is an optional feature on the low gaiters, but is required if you have chosen a snap closure system rather than a 7″ zipper.

Sew the outer and liner of each zipper flap together 5/8″ from the edges across a short side down the long edge and across the other short side (Fig. 11-11). Trim the corners. Invert the assembly and check to see that the flap and zipper edges are the same length. Topstitch along the same three edges leaving one long edge open.

Choose one gaiter to be the right-leg gaiter and place the open edge of the zipper flap along the zipper teeth of the outer seam side of this gaiter, right sides together. (Note: The zipper flaps are sewn to the pants outseam side and snap to the inseam side of each gaiter.)

Sew the flap to the gaiter, right sides together, 5/8″ from the aligned edges. Fold the flap toward the zipper teeth and topstitch 1/4″ from the fold through all thicknesses. Trim the excess of flap seam allowance to prevent its being snarled in the zipper teeth. Repeat for the other gaiter, again making the flap open toward the inseam side of the leg.

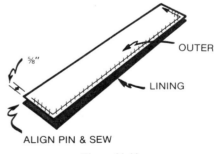

Figure 11-11

Adding Grommets, Hooks, and Snaps (High Gaiters)

(Note: For low gaiters skip to the next section.)
Stretch and smooth the lower gaiter edges to distribute

the elastic evenly. Using a 1/4″ metal rod or a large nail heated over a flame (use a pliers to hold it), make a puncture hole at each of the side angles in both gaiters (Fig. 11-12). Use some care to avoid stretching the elastic after this step, as it has been weakened. Insert a grommet, smooth side out, into each hole and hammer it home. This will clinch the melted edges of the elastic and restore its strength.

At the center front of each gaiter a boot lace hook is installed to prevent snow from being forced up the laces (Fig. 11-12). A Dritz brand package of coat hooks and eyes contains four tough hooks that are easily sewn in place in this application. Alternatively, a cobbler can install a grommet-like hook if you stiffen the area with a leather patch and penetrate all layers with a round hole of 1/8″ diameter. Be certain he understands that the hook is to hold the gaiter *down* and is to be installed on the lining side.

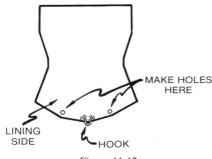

Figure 11-12

Four snaps or Velcro piece sets should be installed at equal intervals along the zipper flaps (Fig. 11-13). These will prevent snow being driven into the zipper, perhaps to freeze the zipper closed (nylon zippers are highly resistant to this fate, metal zippers are more susceptible). First install the female part of each snap set with the decorative side out on the flap.

Mark the locations on the gaiter body and then install the male units. Holes can be melted through the fabric to facilitate installation.

A 1/8″ cord tied through the grommets across the instep concludes the construction of the high gaiters.

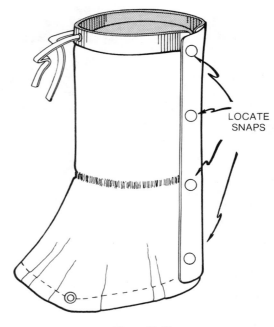

Figure 11-13

Adding Grommets, Hooks, and Snaps (Low Gaiters)

The low gaiters are held in place over the boot by an instep cord tied through two 1/4″ grommets: one on each side about 4″ from each zipper edge. Shift the elastic in the lower sleeve until it is evenly distributed, then pin the points where the grommets will penetrate. Use a flame heated nail or rod held in a pliers to pierce the sleeve and elastic, then install the grommets, smooth side out.

Install a coat hook or shoemaker's boot hook at the outer front of each gaiter, as described in the preceding section.

Three snap sets or 1″ Velcro piece sets should be installed on the zipper flap, if it is used. Space them equally about 1/4″ from the top-stitched edge. A full discussion of the snap placement and installation will be found in the foregoing section.

Chapter 12
Mitten Shells

The mitten shells described in this chapter are a valuable cold weather accessory. The hands, feet, and head are the primary body heat radiators. For comfort in the cold they must be adequately insulated. Moreover, the insulation covering the head and hands must be adjustable in response to body heat generation and environmental temperature; the hiker's feet are usually encased in boots and cannot be adjusted for heat loss. By layering the insulation, the greatest adjustability with the least weight can be achieved. Hat-and-hood seems to be the system of choice for the head; the mitten shells are intended as the outermost layer for the hands.

Choosing Fabrics

For use on ski-tow ropes, belaying practice, etc., I suggest fairly heavy leather of moderate stiffness for the palms, cordura nylon (seven to eleven ounces per square yard) or softer leather for the backs and cordura for the skirts. For ski touring or snowshoeing, light, soft, glove leather palms will feel good and last long. Backs and skirts can be of cordura or preferably of uncoated taffeta or ripstop nylon for lightness and "breathability." Light nylon may be used exclusively if the mitten shells will be used only as hand warmers.

Materials

> 8″ × 24″ leather or cordura nylon (palms and thumbs)
>
> 1/3 yard 44″ uncoated nylon (backs and skirts)
>
> 1-2/3 yards 3/8″ or 1/4″ soft elastic
>
> 1/2 yard 44″ lining fabric (optional)

The most economical way to purchase leather for the palms, thumb pieces, and heel overlap patches is to cut out the pattern pieces full size, and take them along when you shop. Hobbycraft shops and some yard good stores are the most likely sources of glove-weight leather. A discarded leather jacket, skirt, or vest may even provide you with "free" leather for the mitten shells. Check in the closet first, then consider a Goodwill or other used clothing store.

In any use where the heel of the hand and palm may be worn or torn (for example, handling skis or climbing ropes, ski poles, or reins) you should include the heel overlap patch that extends around the mitten back. Use leather for this patch and use double leather layers if you expect hard use.

Sizes and Pattern-Making

Measure the hand size: length and width at the widest point, excluding the thumb.

Begin the back piece pattern by drawing two perpendicular, crossed center lines on a piece of newspaper. Add 1-1/2″ to the hand length measurement. Call this dimension "A" and mark it on one of the center-lines (Fig. 12-1a).

Add 1-3/4″ to the hand width measurement. Call this dimension "B" and mark it on the other centerline (Fig. 12-1a).

Draw two sides parallel to "A" and touching the ends of "B". The top end of the pattern is a semi-circle with a radius of one-half "B" that touches the two sides and the top end of line "A" (see Fig. 12-1b). Cut out this back-piece pattern.

Lay the mitten back-piece on another piece of newspaper and draw its outline. This second pattern piece will be the palm; it must be altered by drawing in and cutting out the thumb "face" as shown in Fig. 12-2.

Locate the dot that will determine the position of the thumb face three-eighths of the distance "A" from the

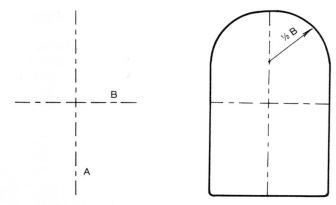

Figure 12-1a & b

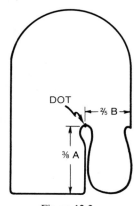

Figure 12-2

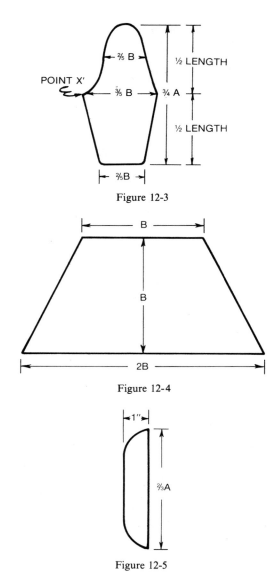

Figure 12-3

Figure 12-4

Figure 12-5

lower edge and two-fifths of the distance "B" across the width of the pattern piece.

Sketch in the thumb shape and curves shown. Trim away the excess 1/2″ length from the non-thumb part of the palm piece.

The thumb-back piece is cut to the shape shown in Fig. 12-3 with the dimensions shown. It is, and should be, much broader than the palmar surface of the thumb.

The mitten skirt patterns are identical on palm and back. They are cut as simple trapezoids with the dimensions shown in Fig. 12-4.

The heel overlap patch (optional) can be cut from scrap leather. It should be approximately 1″ in width, but its length and shape may vary according to the mitten size and scraps available (Fig. 12-5).

Cutting Out

Cut out right hand and left hand palms, backs, and thumbs, then cut four identical skirt pieces and two identical heel overlap patches (optional). Cutting out the leather pieces is best done by taping the pattern pieces in place on the back (rough) surface of the leather and outlining with ink or marking pen. The cutting can then be done with an X-acto knife, single-edge razor blade, or sharp scissors, and the pattern saved for future use.

Constructing the Mitten Shells

Construction should begin with the palm-thumb seam. (Note: Pinning should be avoided in leather.) With the right sides together, align the points X-X′ (see Fig. 12-6). Begin sewing at these points 1/4″ from the cut edges of the

72

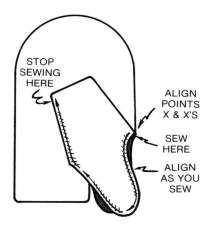

Figure 12-6

leather with the palm piece on the bottom. Continue across the tip of the thumb and on down to the raw wrist edge, aligning and pushing the excess out of the way as you go. Turn the thumb right side out over a pencil eraser.

The palm surface skirt piece can now be sewn to align the skirt and palm pieces, right sides together as shown in Fig. 12-7.

Sew 3/8″ from the aligned edges. Fold the cuff down covering the seam and top-stitch 1/4″ from this first seam (i.e., 1/8″ from the raw edge of the leather [Fig. 12-8]).

Repeat these steps for the other palm, thumb, and skirt piece. Sew the mitten shell backs to their skirt pieces, respectively, using the procedure described above for the palm skirt seams.

If you wish to add the heel overlap patch to reinforce the heel edge of the mitten shell, do it at this time. Place the wrong side of the patch against the right side of the mitten back piece. Align the straight edges, locating the

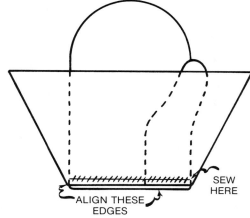

Figure 12-7

wrist end of the patch about 1″ from the raw wrist edge of the back piece (Fig. 12-9).

Topstitch the patch in place 1/8″ from the raw leather edges of the patch. Repeat for the other back piece and patch (remember to locate the patch on the heel side of the other back piece).

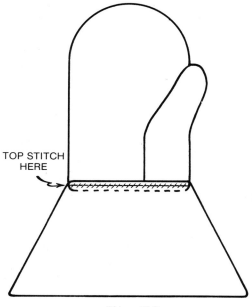

Figure 12-8

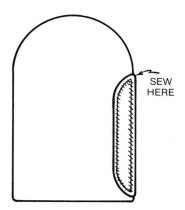

Figure 12-9

Installing the Elastic Bands

To keep out snow and wind the mitten shells are equipped with two elastic bands, one at the wrist, and the other at the skirt edge.

In preparation for installing these bands, the back and

palm pieces of both mitten shells must be sewn together along their heel sides from the lower edge of the skirt to about half way up the hand.

Align the skirt edges along the heel side, with right sides together, and sew the skirt pieces together with a seam 1/2" from the skirt piece edges (Fig. 12-10).

Continue the seam, joining the palm and back pieces along the heel edge at about one-half the length of the palm piece (see Fig. 12-10). Backstitch and remove the assembly from the sewing machine.

On the wrong side of the skirt, mark with chalk along a line 3/4" toward the skirt from the raw palm edge. Continue this line on the backskirt across the width of both skirts (Fig. 12-11). Mark another such line 3/4" from the raw skirt edges. Repeat these steps for the other hand pieces.

Cut two pieces of 1/4"- or 3/8"-wide soft elastic pieces, to be 1-1/2" (2" for a child) longer than your wrist circumference.

Cut two more pieces of the same elastic to a length sufficient to wrap snugly around your arm in your usual winter jacket at a distance "B" above your wrist. Mark the center of each elastic piece.

Leaving a 1/4" "tail," pin one end of a short elastic in place 1/2" from the raw skirt edge at the thumb side of the short chalk line. Pin the midpoint of the elastic to the heel

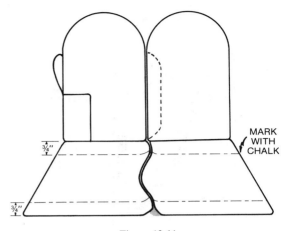

Figure 12-11

edge seam (fold the seam allowances down out of the way). See Fig. 12-12.

Stretch the elastic until it lies along the chalk line which is pulled taut beneath it, and sew. Use a zigzag stitch, if you have one available. If not, sew along the stretched elastic twice with a straight stitch. Continue the seams from the heel seam line to the other end of the chalk line, stretching and sewing. Again leave a 1/4" tail to be caught into the thumb edge seam.

Sew the remaining three elastic pieces in the same fashion.

Fold the raw skirt edge paralleling the long elastic toward the wrong side over the elastic and sew it while stretching the skirt fabric taut. This will form a tube enclosing the elastic (Fig. 12-13).

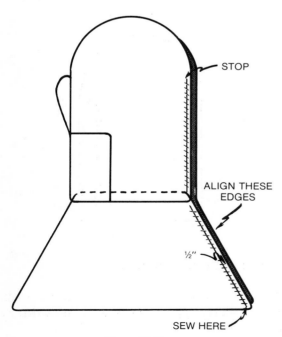

Figure 12-10

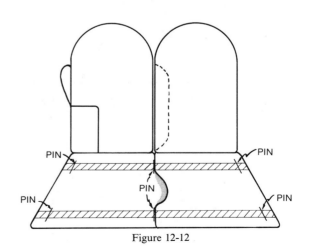

Figure 12-12

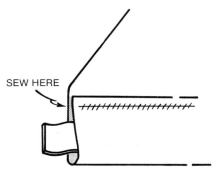

SEW HERE

Figure 12-13

Completing the Mitten Shells

The edge seam may now be completed by folding the assembly again, with right sides together, and continuing the seam along the aligned edges (Fig. 12-13). If you are using leather for the palm and thumb, some difficulty may arise at the point X-X' (see Fig. 12-6). I suggest that you abut the thumb and palm pieces at this point and *don't* overlap them. If they still cannot be sewn smoothly to the

back piece with the sewing machine, skip this area and continue the seam to the skirt elastic tube. Return to the difficult junction and sew it by hand.

Modifications

The mittens may be lined by cutting out duplicates of all the pattern pieces in a suitable fabric, such as cotton flannel, wool knit, etc. The lining can be constructed using the directions for the mitten shell, then tacked in place at the cuff elastic tube (and at the wrist elastic, if desired).

Synthetic batt insulation cut to the shape of the pattern pieces may also be incorporated between the lining and the shell to make expedition-type mitts. The insulation should be fixed to the lining or outer to eliminate its shifting and causing cold spots.

My own preference, however, is for a separate, heavy wool knit mitten to be used inside the unlined shell. The flexibility of combinations to suit differing conditions and the greater ease of drying out the layers at day's end, are advantages lacking in the unitized, expedition-type mitten. Again, the choice rests with you and the uses for which you plan the mitten shells.

Chapter 13
Down or Synthetic Fill Vest/Jacket

An insulated vest or jacket (sometimes called a sweater) has become an indispensable bit of backpacking gear. With down or synthetic fill, it provides the most warmth for its weight of any garment. Both vests and jackets have become fashionable, and their prices are rising. If you are content with a handsome, serviceable garment with few frills, then you can make your own vest or jacket and save some money.

The vest described in this chapter may be converted to a jacket by adding the sleeves. A sleeve pattern and directions are given. What's more, by circling the arm holes and sleeve caps with Velcro, the vest and sleeves become a versatile vest/jacket—a vest with attachable/removable sleeves for varying weather conditions. Before purchasing materials for this project, you should consider which garment will best suit your needs: vest, jacket, or vest/jacket.

In many active, cool-weather sports an insulated vest has some advantages over a sleeved garment. Climbers, ski tourists, and canoeists prefer a vest because of their need for free arm movement. Some backpackers and bicyclists choose a vest because of its lighter weight and lower bulk. Two factors help make the insulated vest a wise choice when weight vs. warmth must be considered. First, for a modern-design, waist-length, nylon shell, down or synthetic insulated jacket, about forty per cent of the weight is in the sleeves. Second, the torso skin temperature is generally higher than that of the arms, hence the body loses less heat through the arms than through the areas covered by a vest. A jacket might be chosen in preference to a vest where weight and bulk are of less concern. A sleeved garment will also be needed for most cold weather/high altitude trips as well as for periods of inactivity, such as sitting out a storm in a tent, birding, and wild-life photography. The removable-sleeve jacket offers some of the benefits of both a vest and an insulated jacket. It is more versatile and comfortable for a wider range of activity levels and weather conditions. It weighs only a fraction of an ounce more than the jacket with attached sleeves but costs a bit more (this is the cost of the Velcro tapes). Whether this additional cost is worthwhile depends largely on how frequently you will wear the vest without sleeves.

Choosing Fill and Fabric

The vest uses readily-available polyester fill or may be filled with down. The weight difference is quite small (about two ounces), but other factors may affect your choice. Down will stuff into a minute package, polyester will not. Polyester will retain warmth when wet, but down will mat and become useless. Perhaps cost will be a deciding factor. By making your own, you will save about half the cost of a ready-made garment, but a down jacket or vest will cost at least twice as much as a comparable synthetic-fill item when material costs are compared.

Materials

Note: Vest dimensions given in parentheses

2-1/2 yards (1-1/2 yards) $\times$ 44" uncoated nylon outer fabric

2-1/2 yards (1-1/2 yards) $\times$ 44" uncoated nylon lining fabric

2-1/2 yards (1-1/2 yards) $\times$ 44" polyester quilt batting fill _or_ 8 ounces (5 ounces) down fill

10" (4") $\times$ 20" nylon or cotton rib knit

1-1/3 yard (0 yard) Velcro hook and pile (optional)

Five or six snap sets with reinforcing leather patches

Down fill will require downproof fabric—high-count nylon taffeta or ripstop—from a backpacking equipment supplier (See Appendix I). Poly-fill will not readily leak through fabric, so "aspen cloth" nylon taffeta available in most large fabric stores may be used. If weight is no object, cotton and polyester blend or other fabrics may be considered.

Making a Pattern

The first step in making the vest, jacket, or vest/jacket is to prepare a paper pattern to the size of the wearer. The vest circumference should exceed the chest measurement of the wearer by about eight to ten inches. This excess girth is called ease and makes for a comfortably loose fit. The vest is intended to reach the hips. Measure a jacket that fits the wearer from the top of the shoulder seam to the hips to determine the proper length.

Draw the arm hole pattern shown in Fig. 13-1 on newspaper. First draw a lattice of 2″ squares, then transfer the shape of the curve, square by square, to the newspaper. Repeat this procedure to prepare patterns for the front neck opening, rear neck opening, and the sleeve top curve if you intend to make sleeves (Fig. 13-1).

Cut out these curve patterns and place them on another sheet of newspaper, as shown in Fig. 13-2. Locate the arm and neck hole pattern pieces so as to give the final pattern

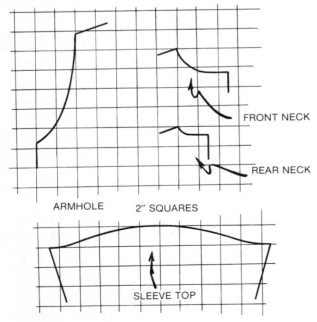

Figure 13-1

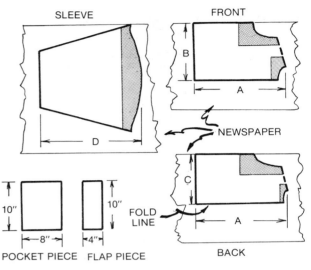

Figure 13-2

dimensions A, B, and C, calculated as follows: A is equal to the measured length from top of shoulder seam to hips along the back of a garment that fits the intended wearer of the vest, plus two inches; B is equal to the chest measurement of the intended wearer, divided by 4, plus five inches (2-1/2″ ease plus 1-1/2″ snap overlap plus 1″ for seam allowances); C is equal to the chest measurement of the intended wearer divided by 4, plus three inches (2-1/2″ ease plus 1/2″ seam allowance). (Note: The fold arrow in Fig. 13-2 indicates that the back piece pattern piece is to be placed along a fabric fold). Sleeve length, D, in Fig. 13-2 is the wearer's outer shirt sleeve length from shoulder to wrist, minus 1-1/2″ to allow for wrist ribbing. The completed newspaper patterns should now be cut out.

Cutting Out the Fabric Pieces

If the lining fabric is placed inside the outer fabric, all pieces can be cut out at once (Fig. 13-3). Lay the newspaper patterns on the folded fabric and cut out the pieces. Separate all pieces and sear all cut edges with a flame or with the soldering iron rig shown in Chapter 2. (Note: All references to the "wrong" side of body and sleeve outer and lining pieces indicate the side facing the fill.)

The collar and sleeve cuffs are made from synthetic or cotton ribbing available in most fabric stores. A 4″ long tubular piece (10″ long if you make sleeve cuffs) should be purchased (the tube is about 20″ in circumference). Cut the tube along a rib and lay it out flat. Mark with chalk the pieces shown in Fig. 13-4 and cut them out. Fold and trim the collar piece to the shape shown in Fig. 13-5. Heat-fuse the cut edges of synthetic ribbing to discourage ravelling.

Patch pockets with flaps are optional, but a worthwhile addition to your vest or jacket. Dimensions are given in Fig. 13-2.

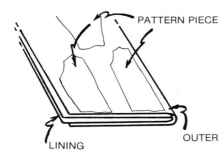

Figure 13-3

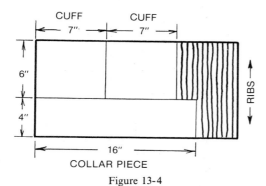

Figure 13-4

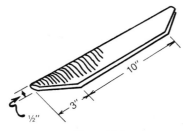

Figure 13-5

Cutting Out the Poly Batting Fill (skip this if you use down fill)

Using the front and back (and sleeve) fabric pieces as patterns, cut out the following batting insulation pieces: two front, one full-width back, (two sleeve, optional).

Joining the Outer Shell and Lining Pieces

Place the right front outer shell on the corresponding lining piece, right sides together. Align and pin along the edges, then sew 3/8″ from the pinned edges leaving a gap as shown in Fig. 13-6. Leave gap "A" if you use bulk down fill, and gap "B" if you use poly fill. Turn the assembly inside out through the gap and top-stitch 1/8″ from the seamed edge, again leaving the gap open. Repeat these shell assembly steps on the left front, back, and sleeve pieces. Leave gaps at the locations indicated in Fig. 13-6.

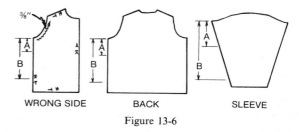

Figure 13-6

Adding the Fill and Quilt-Stabilizing It

Fill material introduced between the shells of a garment (or sleeping bag) shift about with normal body movements and can create uninsulated cold spots. To prevent this, the fill must be compartmented with baffles or quilted to limit movement. Choose a quilting pattern as shown (Fig. 13-7) or design one, and draw chalk lines on both the outer shell and lining of all assemblies. (Note: For neatness, horizontal quilt lines should meet at center front and side seams.)

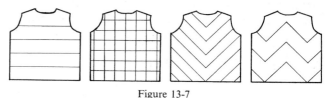

Figure 13-7

Poly Fill Instructions

The polyester fill pieces can now be inserted through the gaps left in the previous step.

Down Fill Instructions

If you plan to purchase down for the vest or jacket, it will be easiest but most expensive to buy individual premeasured packets (Holubar, Frostline). Eight ounces of fill is adequate for the jacket, five ounces will fill the vest. After deciding on a quilting pattern (see Fig. 13-13), calculate the approximate area of each chamber to be filled and divide the total weight of down required into correspondingly small units. Order down packages that come closest to filling the chambers you've drawn. Since down can be purchased in quantities as small as 1/16 ounce, this is a very precise method.

If you are using bulk down, the "handful" should be your standard of measure. Distribute the down into the shells in these proportions: one unit in each front assembly, two units in the back assembly, and one unit in each sleeve. To reduce the mess, work outside on a windless day, and work slowly. Your "handful" will be most accurate if you transfer the down to a large bag or box where it can loft freely.

Introduce the down through the gap you left in the seam, then tuck the raw fabric edges in, pin, and topstitch. Use a strong light source to locate clumps of down, and pull these apart through the fabric. Pat the down to distribute it evenly within the assembly, then pin the quilt lines as described below.

Pinning and Sewing the Quilt-lines — Poly and Down Fill

The fill is now pinned and sewn in place along the chalk quilt-lines. With the outer shell up, pin every 3″ along all quilt lines, starting at junctions. Check to be sure pins pass through the chalk lines in *both* shells. Shift shell fabric as needed to reduce bunching. Check your sewing machine thread tension and adjust it if necessary—equal thread tension will help you sew through extra thickness. Sew along the pin lines. Guide the fabric both ahead of and behind the sewing head to prevent rucking.

Adding the Patch Pockets

Fold and sew a 1/4″ hem along one long edge of a pocket piece. Repeat for the two shorter edges, hemming them toward the same side. Fold and sew a 1″ hem along the remaining long edge, this will be the top of the pocket (Fig. 13-8). Prepare the flap piece by folding it in half along its length, sewing 1/4″ from the short edges, and turning the assembly inside out. Topstitch 1/8″ from the folded and sewn edges (Fig. 13-8).

Pin the pocket piece in place on the vest front. Locate one vertical edge 1-1/2″ from the front assembly "snap" edge, as shown in Fig. 13-9. Align the lower pocket edge with the front assembly edge. Pin and sew around the pocket through all layers, guiding the fabric to prevent puckering.

Place the flap piece raw edges 1/8″ above the pocket and centered (Fig. 13-9). Pin and sew the flap piece 1/4″ from the raw edges. Fold the flap down along this seam and topstitch 1/4″ from the seam (Fig. 13-10). Repeat these steps to attach the other pocket and flap.

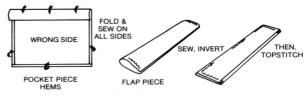

Figure 13-8

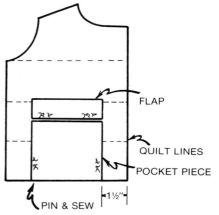

Figure 13-9

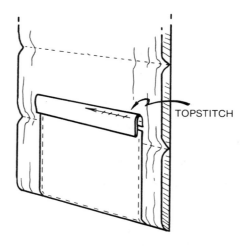

Figure 13-10

Assembling the Vest Body

With the outer shells together, join the two front assemblies to the back assembly at the shoulder seams. Use a 1/4″ seam allowance (see Fig. 13-11).

I. Vest Directions

If you are making the vest, join the front and back assemblies along the side seams. With outer shells together, align the assembly edges and horizontal quilt lines, then pin and sew with a 1/4″ seam allowance (see Fig. 13-11).

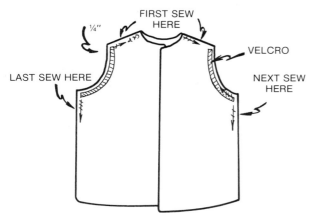

FIRST SEW HERE

1/4″

VELCRO

LAST SEW HERE

NEXT SEW HERE

Figure 13-11

II. Vest/Jacket Directions

If you are making the vest/jacket with removable sleeves, sew the 3/4″ "fuzzy" Velcro strip in place at this time. Align one edge of the Velcro with the armhole edge of the lining of the vest assembly (see Fig. 13-11). Sew 1/8″ from the aligned edges, shifting the rather stiff tape into alignment as you go. Sew the other edge of the Velcro in place, keeping tension on the fabric to prevent puckering. Now sew the vest side seam as described under "vest directions" above.

III. Jacket Directions

If you are making the jacket with attached sleeves, align the upper sleeve edge and armhole edge, outer shells together. Pin and sew with a 1/4″ seam allowance. With outer shells together, pin the vest side seam and sleeve underarm seam, aligning quilt lines as you go. Sew this long seam from the vest lower edge to the cuff with a 1/4″

seam allowance. Repeat for the other sleeve, turn the sleeves inside out and try on your masterpiece.

Removable Sleeves

If you are making the vest/jacket with removable sleeves, the Velcro "hook" tape is now fixed to the sleeves. Align the hook tape with the outer shell surface of the sleeve top edge. Sew the tape 1/8″ from the aligned edges, shifting the tape as needed while you sew. Stitch the other edge of the Velcro hook tape down, keeping tension on the fabric to prevent puckering.

With outer shells together, pin and sew the sleeve seam. Align the edges and quilt lines and sew with a 1/4″ seam allowance. Invert the sleeves and attach them to the vest with the Velcro. Don't resist the temptation to try it on.

Adding the Collar and Cuffs

Locate the center of the folded collar piece and pin it to the center back of the outer shell neck opening, right sides together, raw edges aligned (Fig. 13-12). Pin the front edge of the collar piece to the front "snap" edge of the vest. Gently stretch the neck edge until it assumes its natural shape, then pin the stretched knit collar piece to the neck edge at the shoulder seam. Continue stretching and pinning as needed to evenly distribute the collar piece raw edge along the neck opening. Sew these edges together with a 1/4″ seam allowance, and again 1/8″ from the raw edges.

If you are making the sleeved garment, try it on and trim the sleeve cuff edge 2-1/2″ above your proper sleeve length, if necessary. If you are using down fill, baste above this cuff edge line before cutting.

Fold the cuff piece, right sides together, parallel to the ribs and sew the cut edges together forming a 6″ × 3-1/2″ tube (Fig. 13-13). Fold the tube, wrong sides together, to make a double tube as shown. Slip this double tube over the outer shell cuff end of the sleeve. Twist to align the lengthwise cuff seam with the sleeve underarm seam (see Fig. 13-13). Align the raw edges of the cuff and cuff edge of the sleeve. Place the aligned lengthwise seams under the presser foot 1/4″ from the raw edges. Advance the sewing needle into the fabric, then stretch the sleeve cuff edge taut. This stretch will distribute the knit cuff material around the cuff opening. Continue stretching while you sew around the cuff in 1″ to 2″-segments, leaving a 1/4″ seam allowance. Complete this seam by backstitching over the beginning. Flip down the cuff and try on your sleeve.

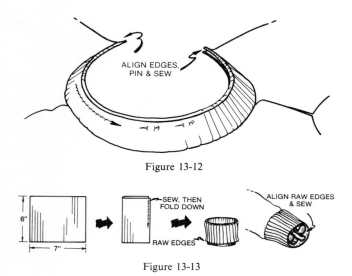

ALIGN EDGES, PIN & SEW

Figure 13-12

6"

7"

SEW, THEN FOLD DOWN

RAW EDGES

ALIGN RAW EDGES & SEW

Figure 13-13

Locating and Attaching the Snaps

The top snap should be placed about 1″ below the fabric neck edge. The bottom one should be approximately 2″ above the vest bottom. The remaining three or four snaps are equally spaced between (Fig. 13-14). Five snaps

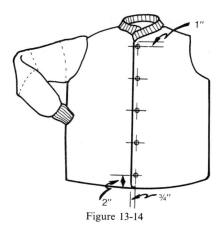

1"

2"   ¾"

Figure 13-14

are adequate for most people, although a very tall person might prefer six. Locate all snaps 3/4″ in from the topstitched fabric edge. Large sewn snaps (Dritz) will work, but set snaps (Durable Dot from Frostline, or equivalent) are much more rugged. Pierce the shell fabric pieces with a hot nail to fuse the fabric surrounding the snap. This will prevent ravelling. A fabric or leather patch on the lining side of each snap unit will increase its strength and add long life. Snaps may be added to pockets and flaps if desired.

Chapter 14
Tent

Do You Really Need a Tent?

In the minds of many campers, car- and wilderness-alike, camping means tenting. The tent is so entwined with their image of camping out that they find it hard to believe that many campers from the mountains and deserts of the Southwestern states don't use one. Many of these arid-land roamers do carry a tube tent, a 9' or 10' tube of polyethylene sheet—12' in circumference—for emergency downpour and snowstorm use. But, otherwise, they confine their hiking to the drier seasons and only suffer occasionally for their folly.

For most of us, however, a tube tent is not always enough. You may need a real tent if you can answer "yes" to any of the following questions:

1. Do you camp where the chance of all-night rain is great? A tube tent or poncho shelter is worse than miserable in a serious rainstorm or day-long drizzle.
2. Will you camp where humidity is high (Southeast, Pacific Northwest, Lakes States, etc.)? Wet gear dries slowly under these conditions, and a tent is the only adequate insurance against wet gear for a whole trip.
3. Do insects present a problem? Low temperature after sunset eliminates this difficulty even in some wet areas, but most hiking areas subject visitors to the annoyance of these vampires.
4. Are any of your potential camping partners (spouse, kids, etc.) deterred by fears that a tent would dispel? Snakes, scorpions, insects, mice, raccoons, etc. may not be stopped completely by a floored tent, but fears of these camp invaders may be quieted. Also, the fear of "sleeping out . . . unprotected" and fear of the unknown will often be put quietly to rest by a tent.*
5. Do you ever camp in a crowd—at a trail head or a car camp on your way to a hiking area—or perhaps even along one of the more crowded "wilderness" trails (e.g., John Muir, White Mountains, etc.)? The privacy of a tent can mean a lot in these circumstances.

If your answer to any of these questions is "yes," then a tent is probably worth considering. Read on.

Make It, or Buy It?

Modern lightweight tents are expensive to buy and somewhat time- and energy-consuming to make. I feel I have pretty thoroughly discussed the joys of making your own equipment in the introduction, but perhaps the tent deserves an additional comment.

If you have more time than money, then consider this: about one-half to two-thirds of the cost of a tent can be saved by doing your own labor (starting from scratch will cut about thirty per cent from presently available *kit* prices). You can use the same materials as the major manufacturers and get the same, or better, quality, with a bit of care. You can also make a tent that will fit your personal needs, and even display your talent with color and pattern.

If you have more money than time or can save enough before your next adventure, then look over the tent lines available. Many are very high in quality and not unreasonable in cost, considering the labor *you* would have to invest to duplicate them. However, be forewarned: Most are highly specialized and may not suit you exactly. At any rate, examining what's available may give

---

* A couple I know has evolved an elaborate ritual: She threatens not to go backpacking unless he brings the tent; he resists on the grounds that it is too heavy, then gives in. She enjoys the hike and the protection of the tent and, especially, winning her annual argument. He enjoys the hike because she has come: He knows that he is the real winner.

you ideas about modifications you might wish to make should you decide to try your hand at tent-making.

If you have the money for a store-bought tent but still prefer to make your own, then congratulations on being a "true believer." Rich or poor, your success will depend on your accumulated sewing skill. But, with perseverence, you can make this tent if you can complete any of the other projects in this book.

Specialization Among Tents

All tents are specialized in function to some degree. Realize this when you search the catalogs, and you will learn much about what certain designs are supposed to do. Note also that *few* tent manufacturers will admit that their products are not "all things to all campers."

In the top range price-wise are the Everest-assault/mountaineering tents. Some of these have actually been used on Everest climbs and stood up to amazing conditions of wind and ice, untended for weeks at a time. At the other end of the scale is the plastic tube tent which will last two or three long trips when made of 4-mil polyethylene, and two or three rainy nights when made of thinner stuff.

In between, in price and weight, there are coated tents for rain and tents with a roof of netting to keep bugs out. There are aerodynamic tents for strong winds, Egyptian cotton tents for traditionalists, double-wall tents for ski expeditions, narrow tents, round tents, cathedral-roofed tents, stand-up tents, bottomless tents, and even a tent of ten baffled layers that purports to let you do without a sleeping bag (from Stevenson/Warmlite). All of these tents can be backpacked and most are light enough to be considered backpacking tents (about three pounds per person is the usual figure stated).

What This Tent Does Well

The tent plan described below is specialized, too. The three central themes in its make-up are: (1) simplicity of construction, (2) light weight, tempered by adequate room for two, and (3) reasonable cost (frills eliminated).

When properly made and sealed, and covered with the rain fly, the tent will keep two people dry and reasonably sane in a two- or three-day rainstorm. With or without the fly, it will keep you about ten degrees warmer than your sleeping bag alone. It is a wonderful haven from bugs and prying eyes. On a chill and blustery lay-over day, it offers a cheerful and bright retreat, a place to read or write or talk, away from the buffeting of the wind.

What This Tent Cannot Do

Since this tent is special in several ways, it becomes necessary to consider what it *won't* do. To disregard these considerations would be to mislead you, the reader.

This tent will not sleep three comfortably, even three eight-year-olds. It is not "rugged" in the Boy Scout sense, nor in the mountain-tent sense, though you can expect it to last many years with only moderate care. The tent will not keep you cool in direct sun (but the fly may), nor is it suited to camping on a glacier (though with proper insulation you can certainly use it on snow, occasionally). It will not keep out bears nor even persistent chipmunks, so hang your food high in a tree; it's safer there anyway.

With these rather obvious limitations out of the way, let's consider some adaptations that make this tent unique, and suit it especially to backpacking use.

Unusual Features of This Tent

This tent has some features not found elsewhere. When you understand the rationale for their inclusion in the design, you will be better prepared to evaluate their usefulness in your version.

Moisture is the camper's enemy. Wet gear and wet skin usually mean discomfort, chill, and even *danger* in the form of hypothermia. The backpacker is particularly vulnerable because of his inability to retreat rapidly to civilization in the event of a drenching rain, dunking, or snow.

Tents are subject to moisture from two sources: precipitation and humidity from the outside, and perspiration from the inhabitants. Tent design must cope with both.

This tent is provided with a fly, that is, a second (waterproof) nylon roof overlying the (permeable) sewn-on one. The permeable "under"-roof permits body moisture (up to one quart per day per person) to escape, while the "over"-roof intercepts raindrops which would quickly saturate the "under"-roof.

Moisture buildup and condensation on the inside are diminished by the large screened surfaces of the tent. Full screen doors and a large rear window, both easily secured against blowing rain by waterproof flaps, provide enough fresh air to keep things dry even during a long drizzle.

While large screen areas and a fly are surely an advantage on a tent, they are certainly nothing new. *This* rain fly, on the other hand, is a real innovation, and I hope you will consider making it even if you will use it only occasionally. Its uniqueness is that it zips together from two ponchos (see Chapter 15). Thus, it serves two functions and saves approximately one pound in the pack (assuming the hiker carries a poncho anyway). It can also be erected without the tent for an emergency rain shelter.

The only other deviation from the usual backpack tent construction is the extensive use of Velcro closures in lieu of zippers, snaps, etc. This lightens the tent, simplifies its construction, and makes it more easily adjusted.

What You'll Need to Make the Tent

Listed below are the materials needed to complete the basic tent (for poncho-rainfly materials, see the next chapter). Add to this list one moderate-sized open space twelve feet by ten feet for laying out, cutting, and pinning, and you're ready to begin!

Materials:

Uncoated ripstop

Coated ripstop

Nylon net screening

Eight feet of 1/16″ × 1″ nylon strap

Eight feet of 1/16″ × 1/2″ nylon strap

Three yards polyester twill tape (1/2″ wide)

Eighty feet of 1/8″ light nylon cord (braided)

Four feet nylon lace, 3/8″ wide × 1/16″ Electric iron

Eighteen inches of 1/16″ × 1-1/2″ nylon strap

Tools:

Sewing machine

7/16″ (#3) grommet setting tool (optional)

Two yardsticks and one 12″ ruler

Candle and/or matches

Scissors (sharp)

Washable "magic" marker

K-Kote (or similar) seam sealer

Accessories:

Fourteen tent stakes or pegs

Eleven 12″ tent pole sections single-end

Two 12″ tent pole sections double-end

Velcro tape (hooks and fuzzy)

Pole top fittings (2)

1/8″ rubber bands (optional)

Nylon thread (available from Frostline in colors)

Order whatever of the above items you will need from the mail order suppliers listed, if you cannot obtain them locally. Expect about two to three weeks delivery time, and two to three weeks of spare time spent in construction. A good job will take longer, so allow for it.

Making the Floor

The floor/sidewall assembly forms a tub-like container for you and your gear. Begin construction by cutting out the main floor piece, "A", and the two sidewall pieces, "B", as shown in Fig. 14-1. The floor sidewall seams are sewn with seam allowances outside: This method will discourage water entry. Lay the long edge of one sidewall "B" against the side edge of the tent bottom "A" wrong (rough) sides together. One inch of piece "B" will extend beyond each slit. Pin and sew 1″ from the raw edges (Fig. 14-2). Fold the seam allowances toward the sidewall as shown in Fig. 14-3 and sew. Repeat these steps for the other sidewall piece. Thoroughly seal the insides and outsides of these seams with K-Kote or equivalent.

The tent floor front end, in front of the slits near the wider end of the floor, is now hemmed 1″ toward the wrong (rough) side. Fold, pin, and sew this hem (Fig. 14-4).

The rear corner stake loops are installed as the corners are closed. Fold the rear edge of sidewall "B" against the diagonal edge of the rear floor, right (slick) sides together. Insert a 6″ piece of 1/2″ nylon webbing, folded, between these edges in the crotch of the fabric fold. Align the raw edges of the webbing piece with the fabric raw edges (Fig. 14-5). Pin and sew this seam with a 1″ seam allowance. Triple-stitch over the webbing ends and stop 1″ from the fabric corners.

Joining the Tent Canopy Pieces

(Note: All future "handed-ness" references assume the user is inside the tent facing the door.)

Cut out right-hand and left-hand front canopy pieces and right-hand and left-hand rear canopy pieces (see Fig. 14-1). Right-hand and left-hand canopy pieces will differ only if your fabric has a right and a wrong side.

Fuse all cut edges if you have not already done so (the selvage is already fused). Pin and sew these pieces together, right sides together, allowing a 1″ seam allowance (Fig. 14-6). Next, fold and pin these overlapped

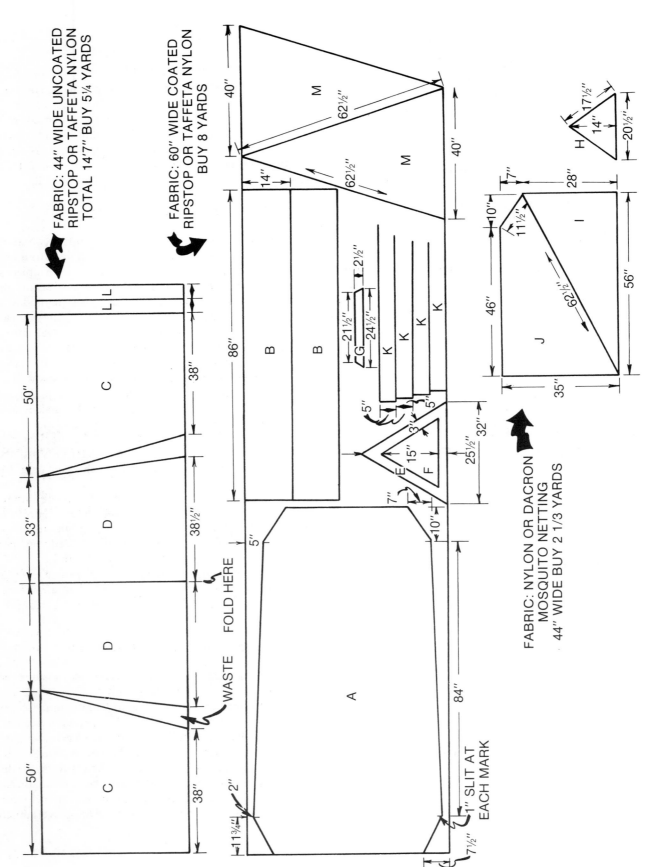

Figure 14-1

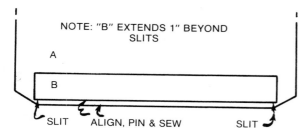

NOTE: "B" EXTENDS 1" BEYOND SLITS

SLIT   ALIGN, PIN & SEW   SLIT

Figure 14-2

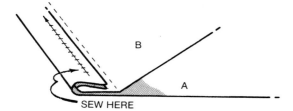

SEW HERE

Figure 14-3

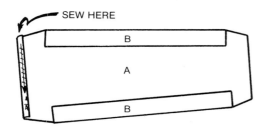

SEW HERE

Figure 14-4

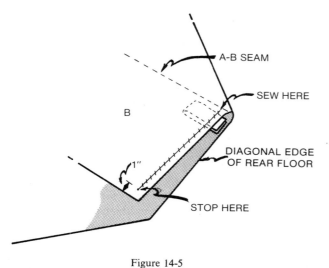

A-B SEAM

SEW HERE

DIAGONAL EDGE OF REAR FLOOR

1"

STOP HERE

Figure 14-5

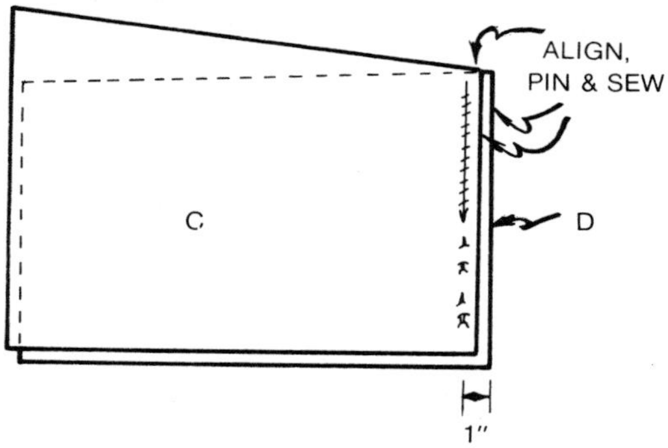

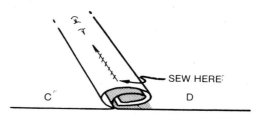

ALIGN, PIN & SEW

C

D

1"

Figure 14-6

SEW HERE

C

D

Figure 14-7

seam allowances toward the *rear* and sew to form a flat felled seam (Fig. 14-7). This will strengthen the seam and give it a finished look.

Repeat the above procedure to form the left hand canopy. Remember that these seam allowances must also go *inside* (i.e., against the wrong side) and be felled toward the rear.

You are now ready to join the right and left roofs along the ridgeline of the tent. This region is subject to more severe stress than any other part of the tent. For this reason, it is reinforced with strong nylon strap and triple-stitched. Take your time here: Rushing may cost much time later.

Using pairs of pins spaced at no more than 6″ intervals, pin right-hand canopy through strap to left-hand canopy, as shown in Fig. 14-8. Begin pinning at the midpoint, carefully aligning the transverse canopy seams. In preparation for sewing, it is advisable to loosely fold or roll the left-hand roof and secure with clothespins: This side must pass under the arm of the sewing machine. Begin sewing at the midpoint (i.e., at the transverse seams) and sew to the front. Do *not* remove pins as you go. Now roll up the right-hand canopy and sew from the center midpoint to the rear end of the canopy. Use a sharp needle and go very slowly, perhaps advancing the machine by hand as you cross the transverse seams.

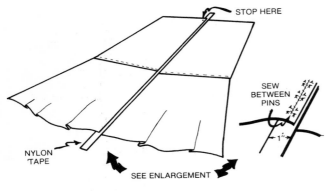

Figure 14-8

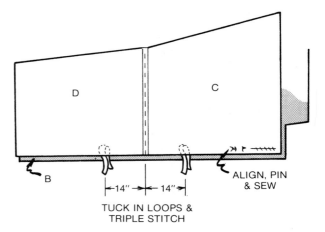

Figure 14-10

Whenever you penetrate many layers of fabric, as at this point, there is considerable danger of needle breakage.

Now remove the pins. Rotate the strap half a turn (180°) so that the strap along the ridgeline is enfolded in roof material (see Fig. 14-9) and pin again, this time down the center. Switch to a *zipper* foot on the sewing machine and stitch 1/8″ from the outer edge of the enfolded *strap*, again sewing from the midpoint to the ends. Since the corresponding seam along the other edge of the strap must be sewn with the assembly turned over, it will be necessary to remove the pins and position them on the new "up" side. If you do not move them, they will snag on the feed dog; and failure to pin is an invitation to a puckered seam. When you have finished, check for gathers along these edge seams. If not severe, they can be ignored.

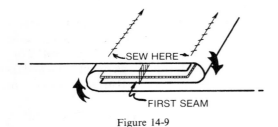

Figure 14-9

Joining Canopy and Floor Sub-assemblies

It is now possible to complete the body of the tent by joining the canopy and floor sub-assemblies.

Locate the canopy side tie-outs by placing marking pen dots 14″ forward and aft of the canopy transverse seam on both the right-hand and left-hand canopy sides. Place the right-hand canopy edge against the right hand sidewall, right sides together. Pin. Fold two 6″ pieces of 1/2″ nylon webbing and insert between the fabric pieces, loops to the right side, at the dots (Fig. 14-10).

Sew the seam in two sections, starting each section from the midpoint. As usual leave a 1″ seam allowance. Starting from the midpoint has the effect of forcing slack toward the ends of the seam, thus eliminating puckered, unevenly sewn, and stretched seams. Fold, pin, and sew a flat fell along this seam, folding seam allowances toward the floor (as in Fig. 14-7).

Repeat above steps for joining the left-hand canopy to the left-hand floor edge. The fell must be sewn "inside" the tent, so to speak. This is made somewhat easier by sewing from the midpoint to the ends, as with preceding seams.

Making the Rear Wall

The tent wall opposite the door is made as a unit before being installed. It is important that it fit precisely in the space allowed. To ensure this, measure the tent canopy and floor edges surrounding this rear wall opening (provide for a 1″ seam allowance). If your measurements differ slightly from those in Fig. 14-11, be certain to modify the pattern size accordingly.

The rear wall assembly consists of three pieces: the frame ("E"), the storm flap (constructed from parts "F" and "G"), and the screen ("H"). Coated ripstop or taffeta is recommended for the frame and flap. This will provide protection from windblown rain. Cut out these pieces using the dimensions shown in Fig. 14-1.

Make a 1″ slit into each inside corner of the frame piece "E" (see Fig. 14-11). Fold each of the flaps you have created toward the wrong (rough) side and iron in place (use very low heat, and practice on scraps first). Pin and sew these flaps as hems (see Fig. 14-11).

The rear screen is made next. Carefully fuse the cut edges of this piece of nylon or Dacron mosquito netting.

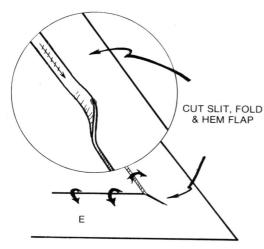

CUT SLIT, FOLD & HEM FLAP

E

Figure 14-11

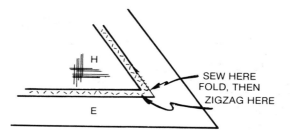

H

SEW HERE
FOLD, THEN
ZIGZAG HERE

E

Figure 14-12

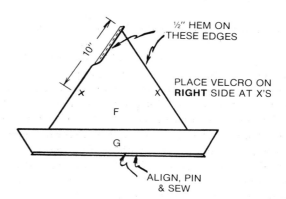

10"

½" HEM ON
THESE EDGES

PLACE VELCRO ON
RIGHT SIDE AT X'S

F

G

ALIGN, PIN
& SEW

Figure 14-13

Pin the screen piece over the inside of the hemmed opening in the frame "E". Try to eliminate stress wrinkles and uneven pull. Sew the screen to the frame with a seam 1/2" from the hemmed opening. To reinforce this seam, fold the screening in, pin and sew again 1/4" from the hemmed opening. Zig-zagging here (if your machine has this feature) secures the screening well (Fig. 14-12). Clip any unsightly edges and fuse with a match.

This rear wall screened window is closed by a storm flap on the inside surface. Make this flap from piece "F" by sewing a 2-1/2" strip of coated fabric, "G", to the lower (longest) edge of piece, along its full width (Fig. 14-13). Give this piece a 1" hem (slick side out, hem toward rough side) on the two upper edges.

Follow these steps to attach the storm flap assembly to the frame. Lay the storm flap right (smooth) side up on top of the frame/screen assembly wrong (rough) side up so that the lower edge of the storm flap assembly is aligned with the lower seam joining the screen to the frame (Fig. 14-14). Pin the flap assembly in place and sew, leaving a 1/2" seam allowance. Trim this seam allowance to 1/4". Fold the storm flap along the seam. Turn the frame/screen/flap assemply right side up and sew through all layers 1/8" from the lower frame lip (indicated in Fig. 14-15). This seam will discourage water from accumulating between the frame and flap.

Three 1-1/2" Velcro fasteners are now sewn to the rear window assembly. Use Fig. 14-13 to guide your placement of the pile pieces on the storm flap. Then close the flap and mark the positions for the corresponding "hook" pieces on the frame; sew them in place.

The frame-window-storm-flap assembly is installed by turning the tent body inside out. The assembly is pinned

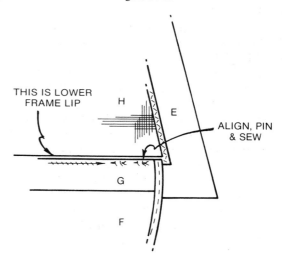

THIS IS LOWER
FRAME LIP

H

E

ALIGN, PIN
& SEW

G

F

Figure 14-14

to the rear opening, right sides together, with a 1" hem. At the center of the floor/frame seam, insert a 6" loop of 1/2" nylon tape, loop to the right (slick) side. When setting up the tent, the rear pole is put through this loop, secure against strong winds. Sew the seam with special care near the ridge tape (if necessary, don a thimble and sew this thick area by hand).

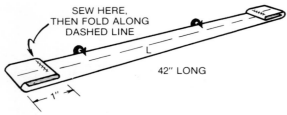

SEW HERE,
THEN FOLD ALONG
DASHED LINE

L

42" LONG

1"

Figure 14-15

The Front Assembly

The front A-frame tent-pole sleeves, front screens, and storm doors are next in our project. Make them separately, pin them together, and they can be attached with one seam on each side of the canopy.

The tent-pole sleeves are made of uncoated ripstop. Cut two strips 5" wide and 48" long. Fuse the edges and "lap"-hem the ends (1/2" folded over and tucked under, Fig. 14-15). Fold strips in half longitudinally with the hems inside and iron in a crease (practice with a cool iron on a scrap).

The screen doors are next. Cut them from netting to the shape shown in Fig. 14-1. Heat-fuse the edges. The bottom and the entrance side of each screen must be edged with ripstop (I prefer coated fabric here, to match the storm doors) to prevent unraveling and absorb stress on the rather flimsy mesh. Cut the edge strips shown in Fig. 14-1, parts ("J") to fit, and fold and press them doubled lengthwise with a cool iron so they appear as shown in Fig. 14-16. Now, join the edge strips to the screen material by tucking the screen into the crease. Pin and sew through all layers (Fig. 14-16). If your machine can zigzag, go over this edging with a wide zigzag stitch. This distributes the stress best in netting. Velcro hook and pile pieces 1" long should be stitched to the screens (Fig. 14-17). With this done, the screens are completed.

The storm doors form a waterproof vestibule at the front of the tent. The storm doors are cut from coated ripstop (Fig. 14-1). Careful laying out will save material. The free edges, those along the door center and bottom, should be hemmed with a 1" hem. Velcro is used to close

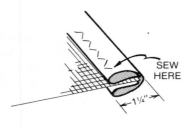

SEW
HERE

1¼"

Figure 14-16

these doors. Sew on only the fuzzy pieces at this time. In the positions indicated in Fig. 14-18, sew an 8" nylon-web stake loop at the front corner of each storm door as shown, for insurance against the intrusion of strong gusty winds. This will greatly reinforce the holding power of the Velcro closures.

The last big sewing job on the tent is the attachment of the tent-pole sleeves, screen door, and storm doors. Lay them atop one another and align the raw edges as shown in Fig. 14-19. Start with a screen door piece right side up,

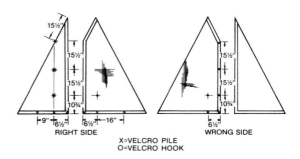

15½"

15½"

15½"

15½"

10¾"

9" 6½" 6½" 16"

RIGHT SIDE

15½"

15½"

10¾"

6½"

WRONG SIDE

X=VELCRO PILE
O=VELCRO HOOK

Figure 14-17

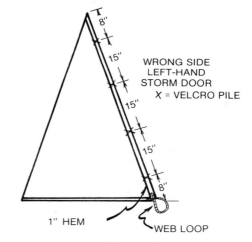

8"

15"

15"

15"

8"

1" HEM

WEB LOOP

WRONG SIDE
LEFT-HAND
STORM DOOR
X = VELCRO PILE

Figure 14-18

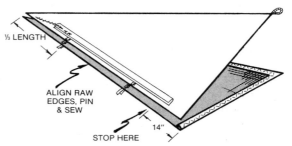

⅓ LENGTH

ALIGN RAW
EDGES, PIN
& SEW

STOP HERE

14"

Figure 14-19

then add the storm door, right side up, and finally the pole sleeve centered along the raw edges. Pin the extreme ends of the seam line, then fill in the middle with pins. Repeat the assembly procedure for the left side pieces: you should now have four edges aligned as in Fig. 14-19. Check again to see that the right side and left side pieces are together and face properly.

Next, cut twelve 4″ lengths of light 1/8″ nylon cord or lace and fuse their ends with flame. At a point one-third the length of the pinned edge, tuck in one 4″ lace loop protruding between the pole sleeve and the storm door, another between the storm and screen door, and a third lace beneath the screen doors. These will hold the polyester tapes used to tie back the doors (Fig. 14-19). Repeat at the two-thirds point. Sew this assembly together 1″ from the pinned raw edges: start at the door peaks and stop 14″ before the foot end. Duplicate this procedure on the other door assembly.

Make up two front stake/pole loops of 1-1/2″ nylon strap 8″ long as shown in Fig. 14-20, leaving off the size 3 (7/16″ inside diameter) grommets for now if you lack the tool.

You are now ready to attach the assemblies to the tent body. (First, refill the machine bobbin—this is no time to run out.) Lay the tent body out, right side of the right hand canopy up. Lay the right hand door assembly on top of it, screen (wrong) side up. Place the peaks of the canopy and door assembly together and align the assembly raw edges with the right front canopy edge (see Fig. 14-21). Again, pin the extreme ends first, then the middle regions of the seam. The pins should follow a straight line 1″ from the aligned fabric edges. Sew from the peak along this line, removing pins as you proceed. Work slowly and watch out for gathering in the tent canopy material. When you reach the end of the seam joining the door assembly parts sewn in the preceding paragraph (i.e., 14″ before the foot edge of the doors), stop. Insert the diagonal edge of the front floor flap between the storm and screen doors (see Fig. 14-21) and pin. Next, insert the front stake/pole loop (shown in Fig. 14-20) between the storm door and the coated sidewall in the lowest point of the corner and

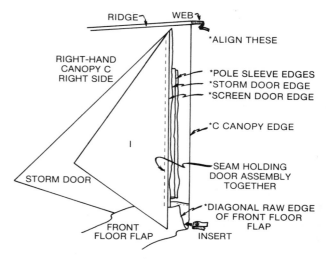

Figure 14-21

pin (Fig. 14-21). Complete the seam, triple-stitching over the stake/pole loop.

When you have completed this seam, take a break; do some shoulder and neck exercises if you are tense. Relax a bit before repeating the procedure for the left hand side assembly. Admire your work—you're in the home stretch.

Upon completion of these seams, you may, if you wish, neat up and reinforce your sewing. Make a few stitches by hand to secure the door tops (seam allowance) to the ridge tape. Then check for wrinkles, alignment, skipped stitches, etc. If things seem okay, proceed by folding the front assembly seam allowance against the wrong side (inside) of the canopy (Fig. 14-22). Pin and sew. This

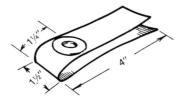

Figure 14-20

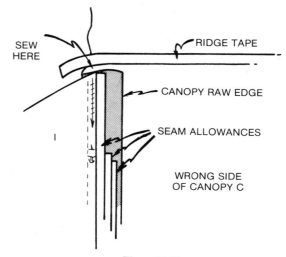

Figure 14-22

felled seam procedure can be used on all remaining unfinished inside seams for a really professional-looking job. It is not vital however and can be dispensed with or put off until later.

The front floor pole loop grommets (size 3) through which the bottoms of the front poles pass can be installed at this time. If you chose not to purchase the rather expensive device (Brookstone Tools) to place these 7/16″ inside diameter grommets, a canvas and awning shop, boating supply, or perhaps a horse tack shop should be able to help. A size 3 grommet is also placed at the front peak, through all canopy and tape layers. The rear pole passes through another size 3 grommet: Set up the tent with poles and stakes before locating its position (approximately 3″ behind the rear canopy peak and centered on the ridge tape). Cut off and sear all excess ridge tape front and rear.

Stakes

If you ordered poles and stakes, as described in the materials list, you are now ready to begin the finishing touches.

I have always felt that available tent stakes were unnecessarily sturdy for backpacking. For mountaineering, in exposed high wind areas, perhaps you need broad, deep stakes, but few backpackers ever intentionally camp under severe conditions like these. My solution for both lightness and ease of erection has been to use tent stakes I made of Kelty 6″ U-loop tent stakes cut in half and bent into a "P" shape in a vise (Fig. 14-23). There are several advantages. First, sixteen stakes are enough to set up tent with fly (leaving two extras); they weigh just five ounces. Second, stake cost is halved (an ingenious soul could cut cost further by making them from aluminum rod stock). Third, these simple stakes go in and out of the ground with great ease, require no tools, and do negligible damage to the tent-site. Finally, packing such small stakes (in their side pocket on the tent bag) permits one to recognize the potential for stakeless tenting. Such tiny stakes, while more than adequate for the floor loops, are unreasonably tiny for holding stressed lines (such as the ridge tie outs) in anything but a light breeze. In a moderate wind, then, it will be necessary to scrounge up adequate dead-falls (rocks, logs, trees, etc.) to secure these vital stress points from collapse. Very quickly a tenter comes to realize the bounty of nature in this regard, and the rarity of the occasion in which more than the floor corner stakes are necessary. Many campsites abound with good tie-out points and carrying extra cord is considerably lighter than carrying extra stakes. My recommendation is to make up or buy a full set of stakes, then experiment to see how few, how light, and how small they can be and still suffice.

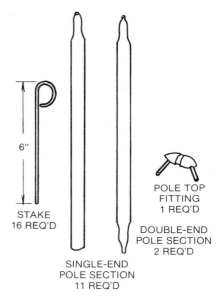

6″

STAKE
16 REQ'D

SINGLE-END
POLE SECTION
11 REQ'D

POLE TOP
FITTING
1 REQ'D

DOUBLE-END
POLE SECTION
2 REQ'D

Figure 14-23

Poles

The tent requires thirteen 12″ tent-pole sections, of which two must be double-ended as in Fig. 14-23 (available from EMS, Morsan). The double-ended sections give two "points" to each front "A" pole. One pointed end penetrates the peak grommet, the other penetrates the stake-loop grommet. If, through an oversight or modification, your tent does not fit this five-section "A" pole size, it is quite simple to add or subtract lengths by purchasing an extra double-ended pole and bisecting it with a hacksaw blade (for a 6″ to 12″addition, you will need two single-ended pole sections).

Many backpacking tents now employ self-erecting poles. Advocates claim greater ease in erecting the tent in the dark or in a strong wind. Since the pole sections are threaded through with 1/8″ shock cord, they are also harder to lose. I am not an advocate: I view any unnecessary form of stored energy in my pack as a potential hazard. However, if I were to make self-erecting poles, the simplest anchor points would seem to be short sections of aluminum rod (old tent stake?) filed to fit smoothly into holes in the end sections. A double round of electrician's tape would hold this pin in place. Examine a commercial self-erecting pole to get ideas.

Another nice touch you may wish to add to your tent is elastic loop stress absorbers in the peak tie-out cords. One-eighth inch shock cord tied into loops works well in this application too. They may be added to the side pole and fly tie-outs as well.

When choosing cord for the stake loops and tie-out lines, I recommend braided nylon or parachute cord of 3/32" or 1/8" diameter. Braided is solid braid; parachute cord has a braided sheath covering a continuous filament core. Both are supple and hold knots well. They are thick enough to resist serious snarling when carelessly packed, and have no tendency to unravel, as does laid rope. Light colors are more visible in evening light and may prevent spills.

A simple tent bag is well worth its weight in protection and convenience. Make it from coated ripstop by the method shown for square bottom stuff sacks in Chapter 8. Allow for final dimensions of 6" diameter by 15" length and you will be able to roll the tent around the poles (packed in their own tough polyethylene bag). Here is a good spot to use up small scraps. Pieced together, they make an adequate tent bag since the bag is subjected to little wear. You may wish to add a stake pocket and perhaps another for extra cord to the outside of the bag.

Some manufacturers recommend stuffing their tents rather than folding. They claim creases wear through first, and stuffing distributes the creases. I dislike the appearance of a stuffed tent as well as the need to compact it to achieve minimum bulk (too much work!). If you choose a stuff method to pack your tent, however, use a slightly heavier nylon for the bag, make its shape compatible with the pack frame and bag on which it will be carried—and, by all means, pack the poles separately.

Setting Up and Completing Your Tent

Choose a windless day and set up the tent in a flat, grassy or sandy spot. First, stake out the floor all around. Assemble, insert, and erect the front pole set. Stake it out loosely; it should stand on its own. Erect the rear pole and stake out its tie. Adjust the front "A" till it's plumb. Now stake the side pull-outs. Crawl in and admire the roomy interior.

Next, get some chalk. It will be necessary to mark the positions for the placement of the remainder of the Velcro tape fasteners on the front floor, screen, and storm doors (see Figs. 14-18 and 14-19). Hold the fuzz side pieces you have already installed in the closed positions; mark and pin "hook side" pieces in place as you go. If you are all thumbs when it comes to hand sewing, ask an experienced friend to help. (Note: It is suggested that these pieces be hand-sewn only because of the unwieldiness of the finished tent under the sewing machine; machine-sewing will work fine if you would rather attempt it.)

Erect the tent again and try the completed door and window closures. Cut twelve pieces of polyester bias tape 10" long. Knot one end of each to a loop in the front door frame (give the other end of each piece a single overhand knot to retard its unraveling). Polyester tape binds well in this application; nylon would slip. The screen and storm doors should be rolled up before tying with a loose bow knot. This will keep wrinkles and stress to a minimum and permit quick and easy release.

The floor and storm-door stake loops will last much longer if each is given a braided nylon cord loop (through which the stake passes). Eight inches will allow for a good knot. A similar replaceable cord loop should pass through the rear ridge-tape end loop. This will save on wear and tear associated with knot tying.

Chapter 15
Poncho
Tent Fly/Shelter-Half

Moisture, in one sense, is the backpacker's enemy. Wet gear means discomfort, time lost in drying out, and even danger of hypothermia if low temperatures and wind prevail after the wetting.

There are three primary sources of moisture to be foiled by the hiker. Dunking yourself or your gear in a creek, lake, or wet snowbank is an unfortunate accident, though it is so infrequent an occurrence that it hardly pays to take special precaution against it. Condensation of moisture inside a tent or snow cave is a more common problem, though usually the amount of water involved is not sufficient to soak gear or to saturate and mat down.* As mentioned in the tent chapter, the solution to condensation is adequate ventilation. Precipitation in the form of rain, sleet, fog, dew, snow, and frost is the last and most insidious source of moisture to wet your equipment. Rain is the most common form during the warm hiking season and also the "wettest."

Preventing rain from dampening clothing and down items can be a considerable chore in some climates. Desert hiking, on the other hand, sometimes requires no rain gear at all! Every major mountain range and hiking area differs somewhat in climate and particularly in the frequency and types of conditions that deliver precipitation. It should be apparent, therefore, that no rain gear system will work best in all situations. This chapter

describes a poncho/fly/shelter-half that has proven effective for my wife and me over a period of years on hikes in the Sierra Nevadas of California, the Rockies in Idaho, and the White Mountains of New Hampshire. I can claim only that it was adequate for us and that it seems light and adaptable. Local information, gleaned from many experienced hikers, is the only trustworthy guide to rain protection with minimum weight in such "difficult" climates as ocean beaches (windy), the Everglades (hot, damp), the Olympic Peninsula (cool rain forest), North Cascades National Park (snowy, cold, foggy), etc.

The idea behind the project described in this chapter is that a poncho is essentially a large waterproof tarp that can serve double duty as a rain shelter. With only small modification, a pair of ponchos can also act as an excellent tent fly.

For rain protection while hiking, the poncho has the advantage of great "airiness." This ventilation can carry away body heat and even perspiration, if the atmosphere is dry enough to absorb it. Many hikers who frequent windy places or travel along narrow, brushy trails disdain the poncho as awkward or too vulnerable to snags. Others, who hike in areas of high humidity, cannot benefit from good ventilation and choose a rain jacket and pants as the best defense against a driving downpour or wet vegetation along trails.

As a rain shelter in camp, a single poncho is small but adequate in an overnight situation but very confining if the hiker must stay put during an extended rain. Two ponchos zipped together solve the size problem. They provide much more dry area than one poncho, due to what might be called the "edge effect." To illustrate, consider a 7′ by 9′ poncho set up at an angle to shed rain (see Fig. 15-1). The dry area beneath this rig is reduced by

---

* Several days stormbound in a waterproof tent, igloo, or snow cave may require drastic measures to keep things dry. One-night camps even in humid places rarely get "wet," though they may get damp. However, some friends of mine tell of their first overnight winter camping in New Hampshire's Presidential Range. Having a cook-hole equipped tent, they cooked soup inside to avoid the wind, and watched in dismay as "chicken gumbo clouds rained chicken gumbo rain" on their sleeping bags. *Always* be sure to provide adequate ventilation, and an easy escape route in case of spilled fuel, if you cook inside a tent. The carbon monoxide generated can be lethal, so consider the benefits of a cold supper if it's too windy to cook outside.

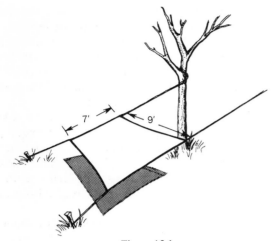

Figure 15-1

the possibility of wind-blown rain intruding around the edges to an area of perhaps 5′ × 7′, or thirty-five square feet, on a particular day. Two ponchos of identical size, zipped together along their length to form a tent-shaped shelter (see Fig. 15-2) can provide more than twice this living space, 7′ × 12′, or eighty-four square feet, by eliminating the "edge effect" along the ridge under the same weather conditions. Even more area can be gained if the additional width is used to lower the outside long edges to the ground to reduce their exposure. You might imagine several cooperating hikers could shelter an entire campground with attached tarps, but beyond three or four tarp units, the weight of "fabric-plus-rain" and the wind stresses involved prevail, rendering large shelters

Figure 15-2

unfeasible and saving us all from a "poncho architect's nightmare" on the trail.

There are advantages to hiking with a poncho-equipped friend or spouse, as you can see. The real advantage to the poncho/fly/shelter-half described in this chapter, however, is that it is designed specifically for use as a pack-covering raincoat for the hiker while hiking and an uncompromised shelter-half when in camp. This dual function item can thus save between one and two pounds in the total pack load. In addition, a poncho pair may be shaped to act as a tent fly for the tent in this book or another similar tent.

The apparent disadvantages of the poncho/fly/shelter-half combination are the inability to use the poncho when it has been incorporated into a camp rain shelter, and the difficulty of setting up a rain shelter when it is raining and the hikers are wearing the ponchos. In practice these problems are not great. A bit of patience in waiting for a lull in the rain is a small price to pay for such a considerable reduction in pack weight. If worse comes to worst and the call of nature *must* be heeded, or darkness is approaching and camp *must* be set up in heavy rain, the hiker's natural "rainsuit" is completely waterproof and always handy; it is also noted for its quick-drying qualities. A quick rinse of this most basic of backpacking apparel will also invariably enhance one's olfactory acceptibility among one's hiking companions.

Other special features of this poncho/fly/shelter-half include a raised hood that will not catch rain when not in use, a zipper ridge with rainflap for fast secure joining, and reinforced grommets for tie-downs.

Materials

(TO MAKE 2 PONCHOS THAT ZIP TO FORM FLY/TARP)

7-1/2 yards waterproof coated nylon fabric, ripstop, or taffeta 55″ or 60″ wide

1/3 yard of heavy nylon, Dacron, or cotton fabric for grommet reinforcing patches

One 100″ zipper (fully separating single or double slide)

Fourteen sets 1/4″ grommets and grommet setting tools

Two feet of Velcro (hook strip plus fuzzy strip) or 12 Velcro circles sets

Twelve feet of 1/8″ nylon cord (face and neck hole drawstrings)

Choosing Materials

Materials, notions, and tools required to make the poncho/fly/shelter-half are listed. Waterproof nylon of two to three ounces per square yard is recommended: Thinner stuff will not stand up to wind stress well, and heavier goods are unnecessary. Either coated taffeta or coated ripstop nylon is acceptable and coated Dacron fabric should make a superior poncho, if you can purchase it. Super K-coat by Kenyon is a double waterproof coating process that will outlast a single-coat treatment. If 55″ or 60″ wide fabric is available, it will save the piecing together work required for the narrower stuff.

I recommend a light color—yellow, tan, or light green are probably best. Raingear may get dirty but is usually rain-washed frequently enough to look presentable, and a dark-colored rain shelter will make for dismal days in camp. Reading, playing board games, cards, journal-keeping, etc. will all be easier and more fun under a light, bright shelter. Also a light-colored fly reflects sunlight better, should you seek shade.

The grommets should be size 0 to accommodate 1/4″ cord and distribute the stresses winds will generate. Large ones are too heavy and smaller ones may tear through the fabric. Make the grommet reinforcing patches of heavy nylon, pre-shrunk canvas, or Dacron sailcloth.

Choose nylon zippers, as they are less susceptible to icing in freezing rain.

Cotton-wrapped Dacron thread is recommended for this rain gear, since the cotton will swell as it absorbs moisture and seal the needle holes more effectively than all-polyester thread.

Cutting Out

Fig. 15-3 shows the dimensions of the poncho body and zipper flap. Cut out one right side and one left side poncho (presuming you want to make a pair) using the dimensions given in Fig. 15-3. Since abrasion is not a

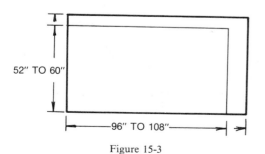

Figure 15-3

major problem with rainwear, we will use the more repellent "slick" side as the right side of the fabric.

If the fabric you have chosen is less than about 50″ wide, it will be necessary to piece the poncho body together. In this case, use the felled seam shown in Fig. 15-4, folding and stitching the seam allowances on the wrong side toward the main body of the poncho.

Make a 1/4″ tuck and a 1″ hem; pin to prevent wrinkles and stitch 1/8″ from the tuck edge. If you are making a pair of ponchos, use chalk to mark one poncho as the right hand and one as the left hand. (In this and all future references to "handedness," the user is assumed to be under the shelter/fly facing the front; poncho hoods are positioned nearer the front.)

Poncho edges will henceforth be referred to as "front," "rear," "zipper," and "outer" edges.

Tuck-hem the front, outer, and rear edges of both poncho pieces toward the wrong side (Fig. 15-5). Make a 1/4″ tuck and a 1″ hem; pin to prevent wrinkles, and stitch 1/8″ from the tuck edge.

If you are making a single poncho, tuck-hem all around and install the hood, then skip to "Sealing the Seams" and grommet installation.

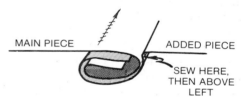

Figure 15-4

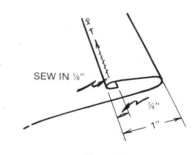

Figure 15-5

Poncho Hoods

Cut the hood main pieces, neck drawstring sleeves, and the edge strips that form the face drawstring tube from the waterproof fabric used for the main poncho pieces. Paper patterns cut to the shape and dimensions in Fig. 15-6 should be made. Judicious folding will allow you to cut both hood pieces with one pass of the scissors (see Fig. 15-7). A smaller piece may be folded similarly to cut out the edge strips for the two hoods.

Hood construction begins with the joining of the hood piece and edge strip along the face edge. Place the edge strip over the hood piece, right (slick) sides together. Align the face edges and pin. Sew around the face edge 1/4″ from the raw fabric edges (Fig. 15-8).

Place a single grommet, size "0" (inside diameter 1/4″),

at the center bottom of the face opening of the hood piece (Note: *not* through the edge strip). Locate it 1/2″ below the seam described in the previous paragraph with its right side toward the right side of the fabric (Fig. 15-8). Now fold the edge strip through the face opening so that its wrong side contacts the wrong side of the hood piece. Pinch or press the seam to fold and topstitch as close as possible to the seamed edge (Fig. 15-9).

Beginning at one end, tuck the raw edge of the edge strip 1/4″ under itself and stitch it to the wrong side of the hood piece (see Fig. 15-9). Continue on around the edge strip, tucking and sewing alternately until you reach the other end. You have now made the face drawstring tube.

Insert a piece of 1/4″ wide nylon lace 36″ long into one top end of this tube, using the drawstring threader described in Chapter 2. Draw the lace through and out the other top end of the tube. Bend a paper clip into a hook and snag the lace by inserting the hook into the grommet. Pin the ends of the lace in place at the drawstring tube ends. Cut a 3/4″ disc from a bit of rubber or leather (such as a tire inner tube or tennis ball). Pierce the center of the disc with a heated nail or rod, making a hole no larger than 1/8″ diameter; cool. Force the lace loop, protruding through the grommet, through the hole in the disc. (Fig. 15-10). Tie an overhand knot in the lace loop below the rubber disc to prevent its pulling out. This disc acts as a friction slide to hold the face opening snug while walking.

Now it is time to complete the hood itself. With right sides together align the raw edges of the hood piece from the drawstring tube ends to the nape of the neck and pin. Beginning with triple-stitching over the drawstring ends to secure them, sew this seam leaving a 1/2″ seam allowance (Fig. 15-11). To improve the watertight qualities of this seam, fold the seam allowances over and sew them to themselves (see Fig. 15-12). The hoods are now complete and ready for installation.

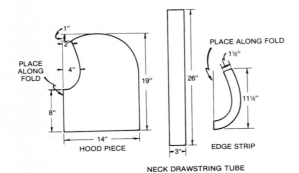

Figure 15-6

Figure 15-7

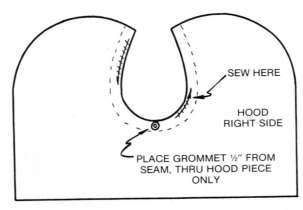

Figure 15-8

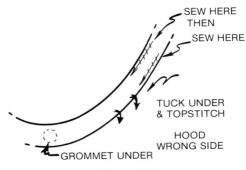

Figure 15-9

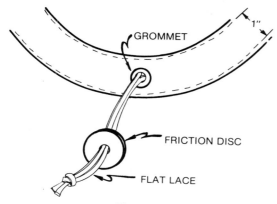

Figure 15-10

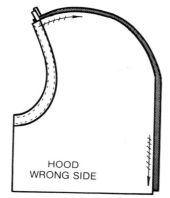

Figure 15-11

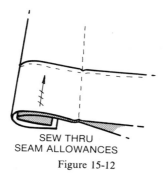

SEW THRU
SEAM ALLOWANCES

Figure 15-12

Installing the Hoods

Draw an 8″ circle centered between outer and zipper edges of each poncho; locate its center 41″ back from the front edge. Place short marking pen dots at center front and center rear, outside the circle, then cut out the 8″ disc. (Note: To avoid errors, place both ponchos slick-side-up with zipper edges together and front edges forward before cutting).

Mark the front center and rear center on the hood neck edge with a dot. Pin the dots on the hood and poncho together, *wrong* sides together; then pin around the circle 1/4″ from the aligned raw edges. Sew along the pin line (Fig. 15-13).

Fold the drawstring sleeve shown in Fig. 15-6 along its length. The drawstring sleeve will hold a lump of cloth, handful of leaves, or whatever, in the hood neck when the poncho is pitched as a tarp or fly. This inelegant device converts the hood neck from a rain-catching depression into a rain-shedding mound.

Turn the poncho/hood assembly wrong side up (Fig. 15-14). Fold the hood/poncho seam back on itself by pinching along the seam, trapping the seam allowances between. (Note: Wrong sides will be out, i.e., seam allowances against the right side of the fabric). Align the raw edges of the drawstring sleeve with the folded edge, and sew 1/4″ from the aligned edges. The feed dog of the

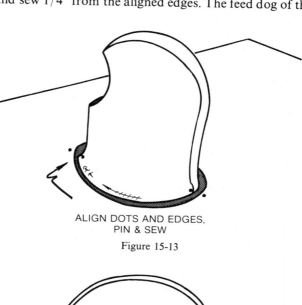

ALIGN DOTS AND EDGES,
PIN & SEW

Figure 15-13

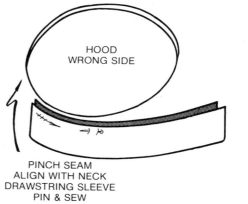

PINCH SEAM
ALIGN WITH NECK
DRAWSTRING SLEEVE
PIN & SEW

Figure 15-14

101

sewing machine must operate in the hood face opening to sew this seam: Take care that the hood fabric itself does not get drawn in. Insert a drawstring lace of 1/4″ nylon and add a cordlock if you wish.

Shaping the Zipper Edges

The quality of the rain and wind shelter provided by the ponchos/tarp/fly arrangement is determined in part by its tautness when erected. Tautness is in turn determined by the shape of the ponchos themselves. A significant aid to achieving a weathertight tent fly or shelter is a catenary-cut ridge. A telephone wire hangs in a catenary curve as does any line of uniform weight suspended at two points. The poncho/fly ridge-line will assume this curve, and, unless the zippers of the ponchos are sewn to accommodate it, the curve will create sagging, wrinkled fabric that will catch rainwater.

To achieve an approximate catenary curve in the poncho/fly/shelter ridge, the zippers joining the ponchos are sewn in such a curve. First locate the *peak points* and draw them in as marking pen dots on the wrong sides of both ponchos 1″ in from the raw zipper edges (Fig. 15-15). To determine their fore and aft positions, use the following procedure: (1) If you will use the fly to cover the tent in this book, locate the peak points 7′ apart and centered so that the fabric in front of the forward peak is equal to that extending behind the rear peak; (2) If you will use the poncho rig as a fly for another two peak tent, use a tape to measure the straight-line distance between the pole peaks: place the peak points accordingly; (3) If the poncho rig will be used only without a tent, the peak points should be placed anywhere from 8″ to 12″ from the fore and aft edges of the ponchos.

Now locate the centerpoint between the two peak points (see Fig. 15-15). Place a chalk dot 3-1/4″ in from the hemmed zipper edge at this point. Draw a straight chalk-line from each peak point to this centerpoint. Locate the mid-point of each chalk line and mark a point 1/2″ in (i.e., toward the body of the poncho) from each chalk line. Using the three marked points as guides,

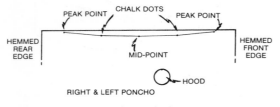

Figure 15-15

102

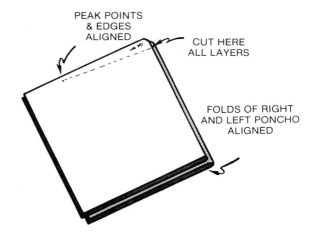

Figure 15-16

sketch in a smooth curve joining them to the peak points (Fig. 15-16). The zipper edges should be cut along these chalk lines. Folding the ponchos at the centerpoints and aligning them will assure congruity of these cut curves (see Fig. 15-16).

Installing the Main or Ridge Zipper

A special, *fully separating* zipper of nylon, 100″ or more in length, should be purchased from a mail order supplier suggested in the Appendix (REI, EMS, or other). YKK Size 5 or 7 is adequate; size 10 is almost too large. Those I have seen come with double sliders and double pulls on the first slider and are intended for sleeping bags. Neither feature is necessary for the ponchos, but neither detracts from adequate functioning of this application.

To be certain that you have oriented the zippers and ponchos correctly, lay the ponchos on the floor, zipper edges adjacent. Lay the zipper in place between the raw edges of the fabric. Position the "bottom" (the end that would be at the bottom of a jacket) of the zipper near the front peak points. Unzip the zipper all the way and place the right hand side zipper-half face down on the right side of the corresponding poncho body piece (Fig. 15-17). Align the zipper tape edge (not the teeth edge) with the raw fabric edge. Begin 1″ behind the front peak point along the chalk line; pin the zipper tape in place. The zipper must end 1″ before the rear peak point. Shorten as required using the method described in Chapter 2. With a zipper foot on the sewing machine, sew the right-hand zipper-half in place, stitching about 1/8″ from the zipper teeth; reverse stitch twice at each end of the seam.

Before sewing the left-hand zipper-half in place, it is

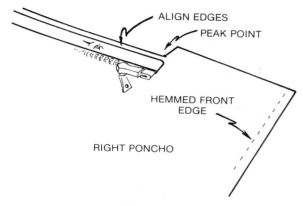

Figure 15-17

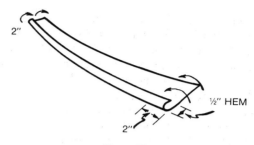

Figure 15-19

necessary to make and pin the ridge zipper flap in place. The zipper flap is intended to keep the zipper dry and thus prevent water from entering the ridge area of the shelter or tent fly erected from the ponchos.

Making and Installing the Zipper Flap

The 4"-wide zipper flap may be pieced together from scrap poncho fabric. Join the pieces so as to form a strip resembling the shape shown in Fig. 15-19, then trim to final shape, using the raw zipper edge of the poncho as a guide to obtain the correct curve. If you piece this part together, lap-fell all transverse seams. (Note that the slick side is up in Fig. 15-18.)

Cut the flap piece 6" greater in length than the peak-to-peak distance *along the curve.* Hem the flap piece 1/2" along the convex curve, then fold and hem the short ends 2" toward the wrong side (Fig. 15-19).

Zip the zipper halves together and lay the left-hand poncho zipper edge on the right-hand poncho zipper edge, wrong sides together. Shorten the left hand zipper half, if you have not already done so. Align all edges and

mark a point near the center of the left hand zipper-half and a corresponding point on the zipper edge of the left hand poncho bodypiece. Unzip the zipper, place the two marks just made in alignment, and align the left hand zipper tape edge with the unhemmed zipper flap edge and poncho body-piece edges. The zipper tape should be on top of the wrong side of the zipper flap (Fig. 15-20).

Check to be certain you have not turned the left hand zipper-half end-for-end in unzipping it; then begin to pin the zipper tape in place, using the pins that hold the flap to the poncho body-piece. Sew along these aligned edges 1/4" from the zipper teeth (see Fig. 15-20). Zip the zipper halves and recheck alignment front and back before proceeding.

For strength and neatness, fold the seam allowance of all three layers—zipper tape, zipper flap, and poncho body piece—toward the body piece (wrong side) and stitch 1/8" from the raw edges. Maintain tension on the body piece proper and the zipper teeth as you sew to prevent excess body fabric from puckering and catching in the seam. The zipper-halves and flap are now fastened securely.

Hem the remaining segments of the zipper edges, from the front and back edges to the peak points, by folding 1/2" toward the wrong side; pin and sew. Include the fore and aft ends of the zipper flap piece (those that cover the peak points) in the hem seam on the left hand poncho.

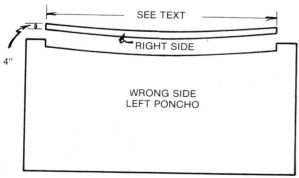

Figure 15-18

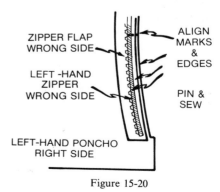

Figure 15-20

In order to function effectively, the zipper flap must be held down against the wind. This may be accomplished with Velcro strips or dots or with snaps. Whichever you choose, locate six to eight points of attachment along the zipper flap at approximately equal intervals. Zip the zipper-halves together and mark the corresponding positions for the other attachment fixtures on the right-hand poncho body. If you use Velcro, put the hooks on the right side of the right hand poncho body (facing out) and the fuzzy on the wrong side of the zipper flap (facing in). If you ever wear a wool sweater under your poncho, the hooks will not damage it. Sew the Velcro or affix the snaps in place, then proceed to the next step.

Sealing the Seams

All seams that require treatment to prevent leaking have now been sewn. It is now time to apply sealant to all fabric areas penetrated by these seams. Check sealant instructions to determine which side of the fabric sealant will best adhere to.

Making and Installing the Grommet Reinforcements

Eight grommets will be placed around each poncho margin. Two additional grommets are placed at the peak points on the right hand poncho *only*. Grommet positions are shown in Fig. 15-21. To strengthen the points where they stress the poncho fabric, a reinforcing patch (covering both the right and wrong sides of the attachment point) should be added as follows. Use poncho fabric scraps or choose a heavier fabric for reinforcement patches. Each patch is made of two fabric pieces cut to the dimensions shown in Fig. 15-22.

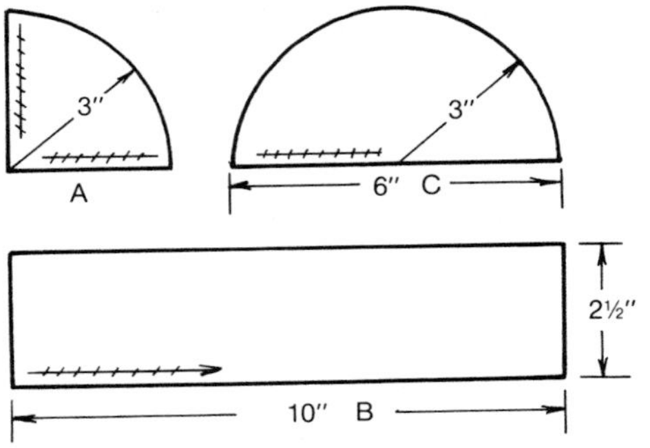

Figure 15-22

Sew the two pieces together along the edge(s) indicated in Fig. 15-22 and turn the patch inside out to hide the seam allowances.

Pin and topstitch the patch in place in the position indicated in Fig. 15-21.

Topstitch the center of a 16″ piece of 1/4″ wide nylon lace to the center of the wrong side of the reinforcing patch at each peak point of the left-hand poncho (see Fig. 15-21). This lace will pass through the peak point grommets on the right-hand poncho and tie to a tent pole peak or other support.

Place a grommet through each of the other reinforcement patches (excluding the patch with the topstitched lace). Position the size "0" (1/4″ inside diameter) washered brass grommets centered and 3/4″ in from the folded patch edges. Fig. 15-21 shows the positions of the grommets in the type "B" patch. If you use a punch to make grommet holes, be certain to heat-fuse the fabric edges created. If you have no punch, grommet holes can be pierced and heat-fused with a nail held with a pliers, heated over a hot flame; a small soldering iron can also be used. Hammer the grommets home with the cast iron setting dies resting on a piece of hardwood to prevent cracking the brittle dies. Check each grommet carefully to be certain that the smooth outside is toward the right (slick) side of the poncho fabric. Try to twist each grommet after it is set: It is tight if it will not twist, but it may crack if hammered beyond this point.

Setting the Side Snaps (or Velcro)

Wind can play havoc with a poncho. Its effect can be diminished, however, by adding side snaps. Though the poncho can still balloon somewhat when the sides are snapped front-to-back, it cannot whip and flutter and block your vision.

Since the poncho you have made is designed to cover a

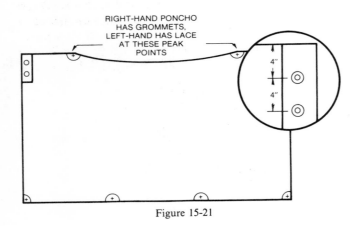

RIGHT-HAND PONCHO HAS GROMMETS, LEFT-HAND HAS LACE AT THESE PEAK POINTS

Figure 15-21

loaded frame pack, the snaps should be placed to accommodate this feature. Fortunately, careful snap placement can allow the poncho to be accurately snapped both with and without a pack.

Use either large, sewn-on snaps or grommet-like "baby durable" or "durable dot" snaps, or Velcro pieces. Put the poncho on and raise your arms out straight. Align the zipper edge and place a pin approximately 12″ below the top of your arm (see Fig. 15-23a). Repeat for the other arm, so that the pin passes through both poncho hems. Take the poncho off and mark the shoulder line (where your arms touched the zipper and outer edges) with chalk. On the wrong side mark the positions for the first two grommet sets with chalk and remove the pins. Call these points "X".

Shoulder your frame pack, with a simulated or actual load that approximates the shape of your usual hiking gear. Don the poncho and mark with chalk the points where the first grommets "X" on the front section of the poncho will meet the back section (these points will be on the zipper and outer hemmed edges of the back half of the poncho); call these points "Y" (see Fig. 15-23b).

Now remove the pack but keep the poncho on. Mark the points "Z" where the "Y" marks on the poncho back contact the front of the poncho (see Fig. 15-23c).

By this rather sinuous course we have arrived at the proper positions to place two snap sets on each side of the poncho so that they will function with and without the frame pack in place. A third grommet set may be added in this way, if you wish, but it is probably not necessary.

Setting the snaps is a snap after all that tedious measuring. Be certain to use only one type (male, for example) on the poncho front and only the other type (female) on the poncho back. Also, be certain that the functioning sides of the snaps face the *wrong* (rough) side of the fabric. The snaps receive far less stress than the grommets and thus need no reinforcement. Except for the problem of Velcro "hooks" catching on sweater material,

I can see no reason that Velcro would not make excellent "snaps" in this application. Let me know if you try it.

Use a piece of cord or a belt to form a fold of poncho against your back when you hike without a pack.

Setting up the Ponchos for Shelter-Half/Tent Fly Use

If you have completed all the above procedures, the poncho is now a complete garment, ready to protect you in the rain, should that unhappy but common occasion arise on your next hike.

To make the poncho pair a fit shelter for you during a prolonged or night-time rain requires a bit more preparation and some practice on your part in setting it up.

Cut some cord of 1/8″ or 3/16″ diameter to be used for tieing out the poncho or rain shelter. You will need ten pieces plus two extra for contingencies. Their length will depend largely on the terrain you hike in, your experience, the height shelter you prefer, etc. I suggest two each of 6′, 8′, and 12′ with six of 10′; try these lengths at first and adjust them on later hikes if needed. Fuse and overhand knot all cord ends to discourage unraveling.

In dry areas it is most convenient to leave the cords knotted to the ponchos. Unzip and separate them to equalize the pack load for two hikers; otherwise, leave the ponchos ready for use as a shelter against dew or radiant cooling or to keep dew off the tent. In areas of more frequent rain it will be necessary to remove the set up cords each morning to permit easy access to the ponchos for trail wear.

A tent pole, hiking staff, or fallen branch can be handy to support the peaks of the shelter in setting up: pad it well to prevent its damaging the fabric or zipper.

If a pole is unavailable but a tree or tall rock is nearby, it will serve. Make a cord loop, place a smooth pebble or piece of bark under the peak or center of the zipped-together ponchos and draw the cord tight, entrapping the pebble in a "bubble" of poncho fabric (see Fig. 15-24).

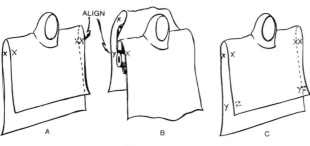

Figure 15-23

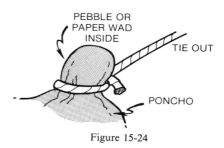

PEBBLE OR
PAPER WAD
INSIDE

TIE OUT

PONCHO

Figure 15-24

Run the cord to a height and fix it; pitch the remainder of the shelter as the scope of your cords permit.

The ponchos may be set up as a tent fly. In this case the tent poles provide peak supports for the fly. Again it is necessary to pad the poles carefully to prevent their damaging the poncho fabric. Use caution in tensioning the cords that support the tent and the fly. Tent and fly should bear almost equal strain to prevent the sagging of either the tent body or the fly. A sagging or loose tarp or fly should be avoided: It is an invitation to wind damage if a sudden gust or squall hits. A trough created by a loose edge can quickly fill and dump water on important gear; its weight can even cause the tarp to collapse. A taut, steeply-pitched tarp or fly is the best insurance of a dry camp.

With reasonable care, your new poncho/shelter/tent fly will keep you dry and comfortable for many years to come. My wish is that they may always give you a lighter pack, a heavier wallet, and the pride that matches your accomplishment.

Chapter 16
Weekender/Soft Pack

Modern lightweight camping gear has opened up the experiences of back-country camping for untold numbers of hikers in recent years. Perhaps the most significant equipment breakthrough in this "rush to the wilderness" has been the hip suspension packframe and bag. Weight reduction realized by the use of lighter fabrics, metals, and insulation were certainly important advantages, but to my mind the shift of the hiker's load from relatively weak neck and shoulder muscles, as in a ruck-sack, to "muscle-less" support at the pelvis, as with a modern frame pack, was the key. Without this innovation, backpacking would still be closed to most of us.

The aluminum or magnesium packframe is well suited to load-carrying on trails. It makes a thirty-pound load almost comfortable and forty to fifty pounds not unbearable for the average male adult. It permits a pair (or more) of hikers who can share communal gear to execute a hike of twelve to fifteen days in a well-watered mountainous area without resupply.

The frame pack is, however, not without its problems and faults. Being suspended away from the body, the load tends to shift and wobble at each step. On a trail this effect is negligible but when hiking, cross-country skiing, or climbing, the resulting imbalance is a significant problem.

The pack and frame is cumbersome and tends to catch on things. Again, on a trail the difficulty is minimized. It is when moving through thick brush or carrying a frame pack by hand, or loading it into an automobile, bus, train, or plane that the problem appears. While much lighter than its Trapper Nelson (wood) and U.S. Army (steel) predecessors, the modern packframe with pack is still considerably heavier than an all-fabric pack of similar capacity.

With all its faults we love it still. The frame pack will continue to be indispensable backpacking equipment and deserves its place on most equipment lists. But a new star is on the horizon to challenge the preeminence of the frame.

A number of recent trends in backpacking and related fields have demonstrated the need for the frame-less backpack to avoid the problems and faults of the pack-frame.

First, and probably most important, is the trend toward more and shorter hiking trips. People are using backcountry facilities for weekend and short holiday trips more than ever before. A full-frame pack and load are frequently unnecessary for these shorter excursions, often in milder conditions.

Hikers of some experience are also attempting to "go lighter." To carry less gear, less food, and achieve a minimum impact on the countryside has become the hallmark of the skilled tramper. There is a corresponding need for lighter, smaller backpacks.

The problems discussed earlier highlight the special needs of bushwhackers, ski-tourists, and climbers: a pack that doesn't catch on things and which hugs the back for improved balance. The frameless pack fulfills their needs. The frameless pack can also serve the canoeist, since it is easily portaged and will not dent or damage a hull. The jet setter who has the chance to fly to his trail head can even fold or roll a frameless pack into a suitcase or duffle bag.

Hitchhikers and those travellers who must tote their luggage on their backs at times and on public transport at other times realize the convenience of a frameless pack in loading as well as in carrying.

If you can find a need for your own frameless backpack among the list above or elsewhere, then this chapter was written for you. It describes the construction of a pack of uncommon virtue. It is light (1-3/4 lb.) and strong. Its moderate size is about right for a five-day backpack or a somewhat shorter ski or climbing jaunt. It is padded against your back for comfort and features hip-suspension and padded shoulder straps. It has a medium size sleeping bag compartment that eliminates the need to carry a separate stuff sack. There are two vertical chambers for other gear, and the pack sports two full-zip side pockets for odds and ends. It can be modified to carry skis, climbing ropes, hardware, camera gear, or what have you. Best of all, it can be made for about one-fourth the cost of a comparable, commercially-made soft pack. With a bit of creativity, it can be modified to fit any hiker or even be made adjustable to fit several different size hikers.

A Word of Caution

This is certainly the most difficult project in this book. However, I have no doubt that anyone who has made one or two of the other projects I have described would be able to make the soft pack. Its greatest difficulty lies in the precision necessary to make the seams meet as intended. I strongly urge you to (1) read the entire chapter before beginning the first seam, (2) to re-read each section before performing any single step, and (3) especially, to mark all seam lines clearly (preferably in washable magic marker or washable ink) before you cut out the fabric pieces.

Allow twice the time you think you will need for each seam and four times as much for cutting out, then mistakes will be minimized—remember, haste makes waste. Take special care in measuring and seam alignment, and your pack will look sharp, fit well, and last a life-time.

Materials

Four yards 45″ wide Dacron sailcloth or nylon pack-cloth

1/2 yard no-wale corduroy

Two yards 1″ nylon web strap material

Two feet 1-1/2 nylon web strap material

Ten feet 3/16″ diameter cord

One leather patch 3″ × 5″

1/2 sheet (2′ × 2′) Bluefoam 3/8″ thick

Two 15″ double slide zippers (open at center)

One 15″ single slide zipper

Two 1″ tabler buckles

One 1-1/2″ clamp or slidetype waist beltbuckle

Two long cordlocks with lower tiedown hole

One short cordlock

Eighteen grommet and washer sets (more for size adjustable type)

Four 1″ clevis pins with lock rings

Special Tools

Thread, hand needles, washable marking pen, scissors, chalk

Heat source, nail or rod, pliers; or soldering iron

Hacksaw or blade with tape-wrapped end for handle

Hand drill, 3/32″ or 1/8″ bit

Hammer to set grommets

Choosing Fabrics

The pack body must be tough, as it will carry considerable weight. The stresses of hiking, hoisting, and packing multiply the dead weight of the pack contents. Abrasion resistance is also required; indeed, the pack is certainly the most abraded of all the hiker's camping gear. These considerations point to fabric in the six to eleven ounce weight range; nylon, 60-40 cloth, cotton canvas (be sure to pre-shrink this), or Dacron. I urge you not to make the pack of flimsy stuff. Your time will be wasted if you cannot depend on the pack under stress conditions. The prototype was made of four-ounce Dacron sailcloth and has held up very well. The use of waterproof fabric should certainly be considered, but be assured that all packs leak through the stitching in a drenching rain. A plastic garbage bag "pack cover" is good insurance in camp.

The back piece (that against the hiker's back) is double thick, and I recommend that it be made of rough-textured absorbent (natural fiber) or non-absorbent fabric. No-wale cotton corduroy, cotton canvas, or rough cordura nylon should work well. The inner back piece is separated from the wearer by 3/8″ of non-absorbent foam pad and can be made of the pack fabric. A non-slippery rough surface is also desirable for the padded shoulder strap covers.

Making Patterns, and a Word about Sizes

If you plan to make more than one bag of the same size, it may be worthwhile to cut out newspaper or muslin patterns of the bag pieces. For one pack, this is not necessary, as the outlines of the pack pieces can be drawn directly on the pack fabric in chalk or washable marking pen. The bag side is probably the most difficult piece to measure for and draw. Use the construction lines shown and use the fabric selvage (check to see that it is straight) as a "base-line" to insure these are parallel. Note that the bag side piece, once cut out, can serve as a template for the other side, but be certain to flip the piece over if you use fabric with a right and wrong side. Similarly, the bag fabric back piece can serve as a pattern for the absorbent fabric back piece.

The pack should fit most adults and teens up to 6'1" comfortably by adjusting the shoulder strap attachment points. If you wish to make a child's pack, all dimensions can be cut down proportionally: The base of the back piece should approximate the distance across the shoulders of the wearer. One-inch webbing should work as a waist belt and 12" zippers are available for pockets and sleeping bag compartment for this smaller size pack.

Cutting Out

The dimensions given on the plans page (Fig. 16-1) are those to the seam lines. *These seam lines should be drawn on the fabric pieces* to aid in sewing. When cutting out, allow 1/2" or 5/8" seam allowance all around each fabric piece.

Drawing the pattern shapes on pack or pattern fabric will be substantially easier if you draw in the centerlines and construction lines shown in the drawings (dashed). Frequent use of a yardstick and right angle (e.g., a T-square, drawing triangle, carpenter's square, etc.) will improve accuracy and prevent alignment headaches later. Repeat: *Do* draw in seam lines shown on plan page; *don't* cut along these lines.

After cutting, there are many raw edges to seal, and they are fairly long. A soldering iron set up as described in the tools chapter is well worth the time spent in setting it up, for this job. Obviously this is not required with all-cotton duck or canvas but should be done to seal 60/40 cloth or other synthetic fabric.

Details, Details

It will be necessary to prepare several small pieces to be added to the main bag at various points during construction. Doing these details first will assure that you have accumulated all needed parts and prevent the frustration of having to interrupt the bag assembly.

The steps described in this section will be presented in the order they will be needed during construction of the main bag. Feel free to by-pass those for which you do not yet possess materials or tools.

Doubling Back Piece

The back piece (the piece in contact with the wearer's back) is double: one layer of pack fabric and one of

rough/absorbent fiber. These large pieces may be pieced together from smaller stuff to avoid purchasing excess fabric. The first "detail," then, is to stitch the natural fiber back piece, wrong sides together, to the pack fabric back piece. The latter must have its marking pen seam lines facing upward as you sew. Sew 1/4" outside these seam lines with a loose, basting stitch, all around.

Making the Pockets

Two pocket pieces are used to form each pocket. Use Fig. 16-2 to locate the inside corners and clip and heat-fuse each inside corner to the seam line. Fold the pocket piece along a line bisecting the clipped inside corner with right sides together: This will bring the two adjacent seam lines in contact (Fig. 16-3). Sew this straight seam.

Now open the fold, and fold the seam allowances from this seam toward the zipper edge and stitch down (Fig. 16-4). Repeat these steps for all eight pocket piece inside corners. Hem all around each pocket piece folding the raw edge under (to the wrong side) along the seam line.

Pin the zipper right side (pull-tab side) to the wrong side of the hemmed zipper edge of the pocket piece. Align the hem of the zipper edge with the zipper teeth allowing a space of 1/8" for the zipper slide to pass (Fig. 16-5) and sew. Sew the other zipper tape to its corresponding pocket piece and complete the other pocket using these same procedures. Zipper flaps of your own design may be added at this time, if you expect they will be needed.

Cut two 4" pieces of 1/8" cord; fuse their ends. These will anchor the cord-locks used to hold down the top flap. Note their location in Fig. 16-6 and insert them while sewing the pockets in place.

Once the pockets have been assembled, they may be installed on the right side (the side with the drawn seam lines) of each side piece. Draw a "rectangle" with curved sides 11" long and parallel ends of 5-1/2" with the top end 4-1/2" below the raw top edge of the side piece (measured vertically), as in Fig. 16-6. Top-stitch the pocket hem in place, inserting the cordlock loop 1" above the lower rear corner as shown. Sew close to the pocket hem, reversing at the zippers for strength.

The Lower Shoulder Straps

Cut two 12" pieces of 1" strap material and melt their ends. These will be the lower shoulder straps.

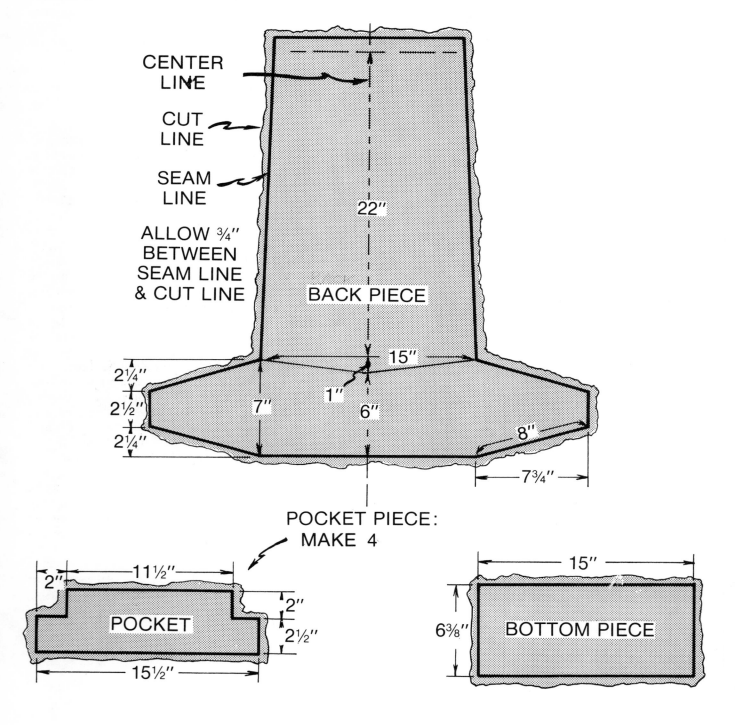

CENTER LINE

CUT LINE

SEAM LINE

ALLOW ¾" BETWEEN SEAM LINE & CUT LINE

22"

BACK PIECE

2¼"

2½"

2¼"

15"

7"

1"

6"

8"

7¾"

POCKET PIECE: MAKE 4

2"

11½"

2"

POCKET

2½"

15½"

15"

6⅜"

BOTTOM PIECE

Figure 16-1a

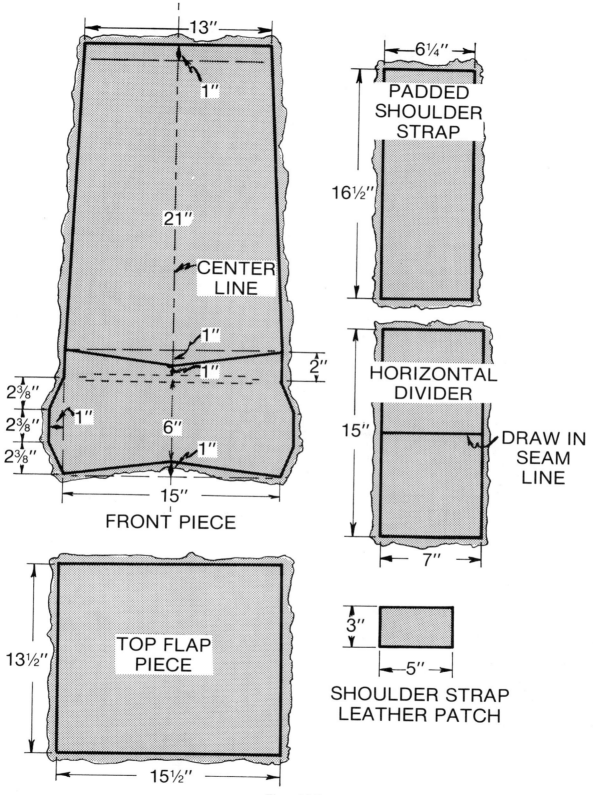

13″

1″

21″

CENTER LINE

1″

1″

2″

2³⁄₈″

2³⁄₈″

1″

6″

2³⁄₈″

1″

15″

FRONT PIECE

6¼″

PADDED SHOULDER STRAP

16½″

HORIZONTAL DIVIDER

15″

DRAW IN SEAM LINE

7″

13½″

TOP FLAP PIECE

15½″

3″

5″

SHOULDER STRAP LEATHER PATCH

Figure 16-1b

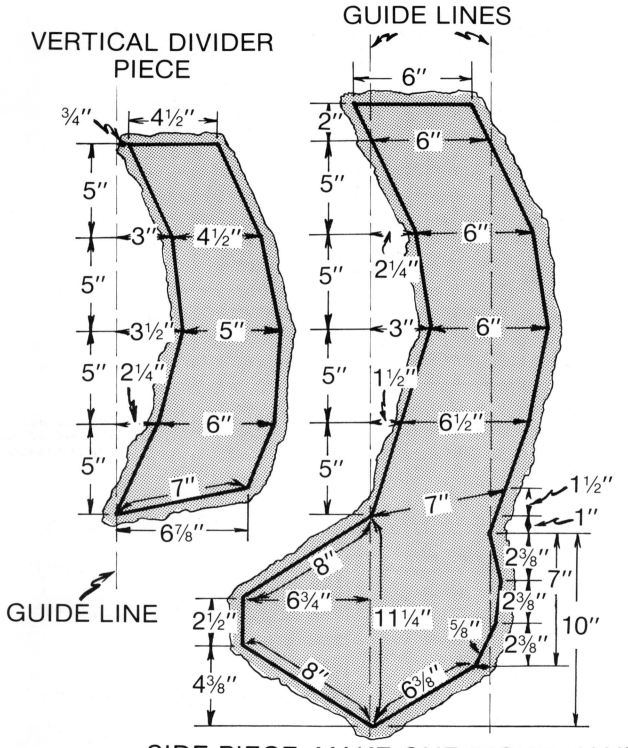

VERTICAL DIVIDER
PIECE

GUIDE LINES

GUIDE LINE

SIDE PIECE: MAKE ONE RIGHT-HAND
& ONE LEFT-HAND

Figure 16-1c

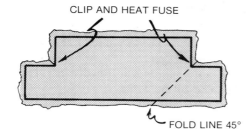

CLIP AND HEAT FUSE

FOLD LINE 45°

Figure 16-2

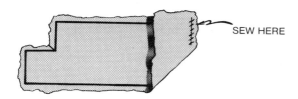

SEW HERE

Figure 16-3

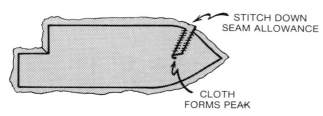

STITCH DOWN
SEAM ALLOWANCE

CLOTH
FORMS PEAK

Figure 16-4

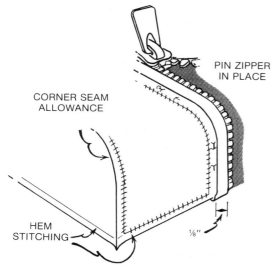

PIN ZIPPER
IN PLACE

CORNER SEAM
ALLOWANCE

HEM
STITCHING

1/8"

Figure 16-5

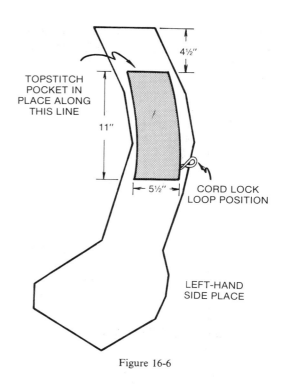

4½"

TOPSTITCH
POCKET IN
PLACE ALONG
THIS LINE

11"

5½"

CORD LOCK
LOOP POSITION

LEFT-HAND
SIDE PLACE

Figure 16-6

The Divider Assembly

The horizontal and vertical dividers are joined as shown in Fig. 16-7. The top end of the vertical divider should then be hemmed. Fold it along the drawn seam line and sew.

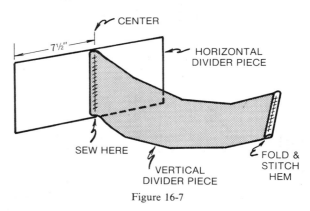

CENTER

7½"

HORIZONTAL
DIVIDER PIECE

SEW HERE

VERTICAL
DIVIDER PIECE

FOLD &
STITCH
HEM

Figure 16-7

The Sleeping Bag Compartment Zipper

The front piece must be slit and the slit edges hemmed for the zipper. Six inches above the bottom seam line of the front piece (measured at the centerline) draw a line bisected by, and perpendicular to, the centerline, 13" long.

115

Using a razor or sharp knife, slit along this line. Cut a 1/4″ long "V" at each end of the slit (Fig. 16-8), then carefully fuse the cut fabric with a match. Fold the narrow flaps toward the wrong side of the front piece and sew, making a 1/4″ × 13-1/2″ open rectangle. Shorten the zipper if necessary (see instructions in Chapter 2) to fit into the slot you have sewn. Place the zipper in position, tab to the right side, and sew in place close to the hemmed edge. Test to be certain the hem does not catch in the slide (Fig. 16-9).

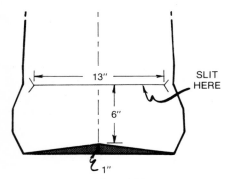

Figure 16-8

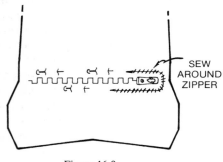

Figure 16-9

Padded Shoulder Straps

Padded shoulder straps are quite easy to make and save a very large fraction of the cost of purchasing them. Here's a simple method:

Cut the fabric pieces shown in Fig. 16-1 from cordura nylon, cotton, or 60-40 cloth. A rough-textured fabric will slide less on the shoulder, but avoid scratchy stuff if you ever hike in a T-shirt or bare-shouldered. Fold each piece lengthwise and pin. Sew 1/2″ from the long edge. Invert over a yardstick. Cut the Ensolite or blue-foam (polyethylene) padding piece from 3/8″ stock (or adjust the size of the fabric piece if you use 1/2″ thick). Note: One-quarter inch padding is fine for a child's pack or

daypack, but deforms too much under an adult pack load. The fit should be very snug; fold the padding piece if necessary to insert it. The fabric seam should lie along the edge of the padding piece.

Fold one fabric tube end as shown in Fig. 16-10 to form the pointed end of the pad.

Sew three times around the edge of this pointed tip and crisscross to form the pattern in Fig. 16-11, leaving the area A for the grommet.

The other end of the padded shoulder strap holds the adjusting buckle. Cut two 6″ long pieces of 1″ wide strap material. Insert each strap into a tabler buckle as shown in Fig. 16-12.

Now insert the free ends of the strap into the open end

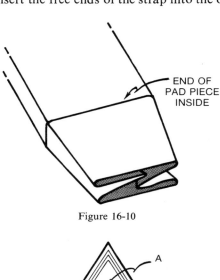

Figure 16-10

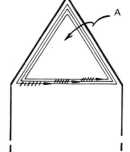

Figure 16-11

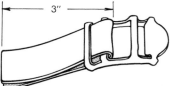

Figure 16-12

of each shoulder pad fabric tube, center and pin in place. Fold the tube as for the grommeted end (Fig. 16-13) and stitch securely using the pattern described for the pointed end of the pad (Fig. 16-11).

If the fabric contains any synthetic fiber, the grommet hole through the pointed end should be heat-fused and the grommet set very firmly.

A lightweight hauling loop to attach at the upper shoulder strap anchor points can be made from a length of 1″ nylon strap webbing and two grommets. Admittedly it is not an absolute necessity but its convenience in carrying the loaded pack short distances and hanging it up between trips warrants your consideration.

To begin making the loop, cut a 7″ piece of 1″ nylon webbing material and heat-fuse the cut ends. Fold each end 3/4″ toward the wrong side and piece the center of each folded section with a hot nail held in pliers (Fig. 16-14).

Enlarge these holes by melting with the nail until the grommets' "male" side will fit. *Do not* insert the grommets at this time.

Fold the webbing along its length and sew close to the webbing edges. Begin sewing 2″ from one end and stop 2″ from the other end (Fig. 16-15). Insert a 5″ section of 1/4″ clothesline or other soft 1/4″ cord into the tube you have just made.

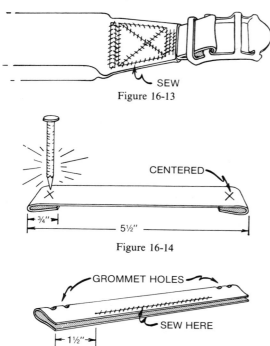

SEW

Figure 16-13

CENTERED

¾″   5½″

Figure 16-14

GROMMET HOLES

SEW HERE

1½″

Figure 16-15

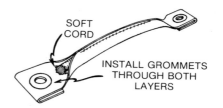

SOFT CORD

INSTALL GROMMETS THROUGH BOTH LAYERS

Figure 16-16

Now insert the grommets and hammer them in place firmly (Fig. 16-16).

The Last Details

Any modification or additions you wish to include on the pack should be planned and executed before continuing. You may wish to consider adding lash points for additional gear, a crampon patch, ice axe loops, or other special equipment hauling facilities.

Constructing the Pack Body

Now that the detail work and accessory pieces are completed, construction of the pack body can commence. The three-chambered body of the pack requires careful alignment and accurate sewing. I suggest that you double check all seams before beginning to sew to be certain all seam lines are marked. Remember that all seam allowances will be inside the finished compartments (i.e., to the wrong side); this will create some difficult sewing, so don't start a seam when you are tired or frustrated. Since the pack will receive considerable stress at times, it is advisable to double-sew each seam, leaving about 1/8″ between the lines of stitching.

Begin construction by sewing the side pieces to the back piece. With the right sides together, align the dots (shown in Fig. 16-17) that mark the angle between the upper back and the hip-hugging "horn" of both side pieces and the double thick back piece. Pin. Insert the 1″ × 18″ lower shoulder strap piece at about a 45° angle from the vertical approximately 1″ above the dots, and pin (Fig. 16-17). Sew the 10-1/2″ stretch to the first "bend" in the side piece, triple-stitching over the shoulder strap end. Without withdrawing the needle from the fabric, lift the presser foot and realign the fabric edges (and seam lines) for the next segment of the seam. Repeat this realigning for the last seam segment from the third bend in the side piece to the raw upper edges. Do not double-stitch this seam as it will be top-stitched later in the construction.

Repeat the above steps for the left hand side piece.

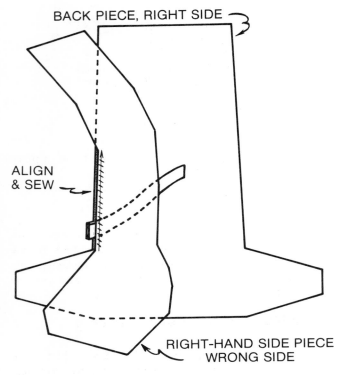

BACK PIECE, RIGHT SIDE

ALIGN
& SEW

RIGHT-HAND SIDE PIECE
WRONG SIDE

Figure 16-17

Adding the Divider Assembly

Place the vertical divider seam line on top of the corresponding "centerline" on the wrong side of the back piece. Locate the lower end of the vertical divider seam line at the point of the shallow "V" made by the horizontal divider seam lines (Fig. 16-18). Pin and stitch this vertical divider in place by segments, stopping to realign the seam lines at each angle in the vertical divider. Go back over this seam again to strengthen it.

Now flatten the lower end of the vertical divider under the horizontal divider and align the seam lines of the horizontal divider with the shallow "V" drawn on the wrong side of the back piece (Fig. 16-19). Sew from the point of the "V" toward the edge. Repeat for the other side, then sew over this seam to strengthen it.

Joining Back and Bottom Pieces

With right sides together, pin the back and bottom pieces together along their seam allowances (Fig. 16-20). Sew this seam, then go over it again for added strength.

Joining Horizontal Pieces to Side Pieces

It is now time to give the pack a third dimension by sewing the horizontal divider ends to the side pieces and the bottom piece ends to the side pieces.

Align the seam line of the horizontal divider piece end with the diagonal line drawn on the corresponding side piece. Place the upper surface of the divider piece against the wrong surface of the side piece (Fig. 16-21) and pin along the seam lines. Begin sewing as close to the backpiece/horizontal divider seam end as possible and sew over the seam again to reinforce. Repeat the procedure to join the other side piece to the other end of the horizontal divider.

Now the bottom and side pieces are joined at their corresponding edges. Turn the side and bottom pieces inside out, causing their right sides to come together along the seam lines (see Fig. 16-21). Align and pin. Begin sewing as close as possible to the back piece/bottom seam end. Again double this seam for strength. Repeat for the other side-edge of the bottom piece.

Adding the Front Piece

The front piece is joined to the assembly first at the bottom piece, then progressively up the side pieces and dividers.

The Bottom Piece/Front Piece Seam

Pin the front piece to the bottom piece right sides together along their corresponding edges at the seam lines. You may find it easier to do the right hand side first, then the left, since the front piece edge has an angle at the center (Fig. 16-22).

Begin sewing at the point of the angle and continue to the end crossing the bottom piece/side piece seam. Repeat the alignment, pinning, and sewing for the left hand half of the seam, then sew over the entire seam again for strength. Note: If you desire to include an ice axe carrier on your pack, an 8" length of 3/4" nylon strap material should be inserted in the position shown in Fig. 16-22.

Closing the Sleeping Bag Compartment

The lower sections of side, back, and front pieces with the bottom piece and horizontal divider form the sleeping bag compartment. Closing this section of the assembly is accomplished by sewing the two side piece/front piece

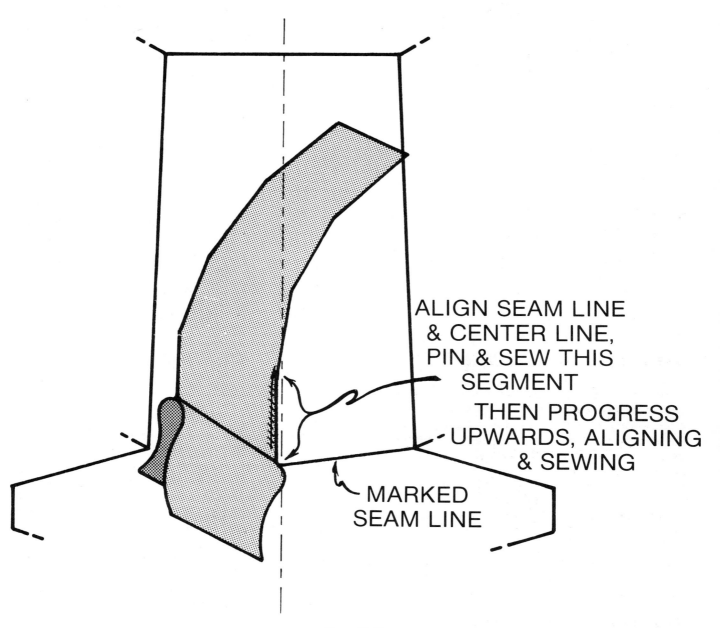

ALIGN SEAM LINE
& CENTER LINE,
PIN & SEW THIS
SEGMENT

THEN PROGRESS
UPWARDS, ALIGNING
& SEWING

MARKED
SEAM LINE

Figure 16-18

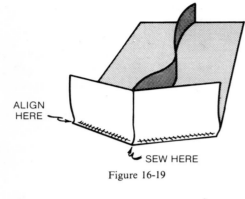

ALIGN HERE

SEW HERE

Figure 16-19

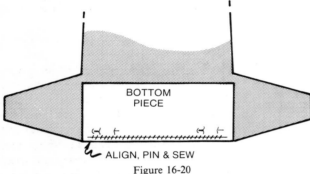

BOTTOM PIECE

ALIGN, PIN & SEW

Figure 16-20

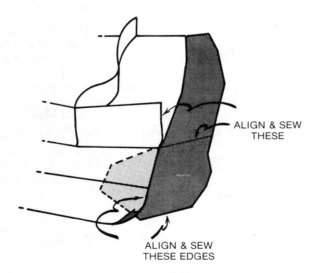

ALIGN & SEW THESE

ALIGN & SEW THESE EDGES

Figure 16-21

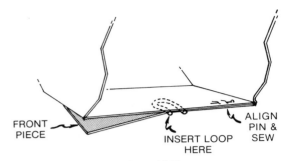

FRONT PIECE

INSERT LOOP HERE

ALIGN PIN & SEW

Figure 16-22

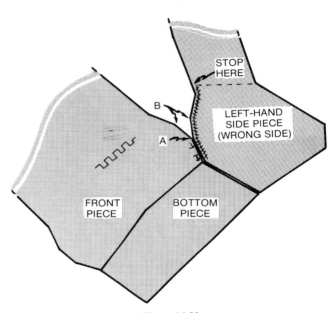

STOP HERE

B

A

LEFT-HAND SIDE PIECE (WRONG SIDE)

FRONT PIECE

BOTTOM PIECE

Figure 16-23

Start the seam at the junction of the bottom piece/side piece seam with the bottom piece/front piece seam. When you reach the first angle ("A" in Fig. 16-23), place the sewing needle deep in the fabric, lift the presser foot and realign the seam lines, if necessary, for the next segment to points "B". Continue in this fashion until you reach the junction of the seam lines with the corner of the horizontal divider. Repeat for the right hand side piece/front piece seam to the corresponding end-point. Double both of these seams.

Now place the lower surface of the horizontal divider against the wrong side of the front piece. Pin the center at the point of the "V" seam line on the front piece. Align the seam lines from center to one side piece, pin and sew. Be sure not to catch the vertical divider in the seam. Repeat for the other half of the seam.

The sleeping bag compartment is now closed.

seams from the bottom piece to the horizontal divider, then sewing the horizontal divider to the front piece.

Place the right sides of the front piece and left-hand side pieces in contact by turning the area inside out and align the first segment of the three angled section (Fig. 16-23).

120

Completing the Upper Compartments

To complete the two vertical compartments, three seams are required: one joining the vertical divider and the front piece, and the two seams joining the edges of the side and front pieces.

The seam line of the vertical divider has two angles which preclude simple alignment with the front-piece centerline. It is easiest to align, pin, and sew this seam in segments, stopping at each angle to align the next segment. Beginning at the horizontal divider/vertical divider seam junction, align and pin the seam lines of the vertical divider and the front piece centerline. At the first angle insert the machine needle deep into the fabric, lift the presser foot, realign the seam lines of the next segment and resume sewing. Upon completion of this seam go back and resew it to reinforce.

The last two seams of the bag construction are certainly the most awkward to sew, though not really difficult. Turn the entire pack inside out so that it is entirely contained in the right-hand upper compartment, which is also inside out. You have done this correctly if the right sides of the upper right hand side-piece and front piece are able to touch along their seam lines (see Fig. 16-24).

Starting at the horizontal divider, align and pin the seam lines just described up to the first angle in the side piece. Sew this segment, stopping at the angle to realign for the next segment. Complete the seam to the upper edge of the fabric pieces. Check carefully that none of the material in the "bag" you have created has been caught into the seam. Now double the seam. Carefully pull the contents of the "bag" out and invert it. Repeat the above procedures to construct the left hand vertical compartment. The body of the pack bag is now complete.

Adding the Hip Belt

The hip belt construction is started with the pack bag right side out. Pull the forward pointing "horn" sections of the side and front pieces through the sleeping bag compartment zipper opening.

Hem the ends of these "horn" sections by folding 1/2" toward the wrong side and sewing (Figure 16-25). Next align the "horn" section seam lines, right sides together, and sew both upper and lower edges (see Fig. 16-25). Repeat these steps for both right and left "horns."

Push the "horns" back through the zipper slot and turn them right side out in their normal position.

Starting at the right-hand horn upper edge, topstitch 1/8" from the folded edge along the entire seam, joining the side and back pieces (Fig. 16-26), from the front of the horn to the top raw edge.

Take pains to be sure that the fabric is drawn tight against the earlier seams and stop at the horn/body angle and later angles to lift the presser foot and change the direction of the seam. Repeat for the other side/front seam.

Using the fabric "horn" as a template, cut two pads of bluefoam to fill the area from 1/4" behind the hemmed horn edges to about 5" back from this point (Fig. 16-27). The pads should be about 1/4" smaller in length and height than the space they will fill.

Taper the front, top, and bottom edges of the pads with a soldering iron or a nail held with a pliers in a gas flame (see Fig. 16-28).

Insert the pads to check their fit; trim if required. Remove them for the next step.

Cut two 12" pieces of 1-1/2" heavy nylon or cotton webbing material (1" is adequate for a child's pack) and fuse their ends with heat. Insert one webbing piece into each horn opening about 2" and stitch in place 1/4" from the open end (Fig. 16-29). Go back and forth over this stitching by reversing the machine stitch a few times since this part of the pack will receive considerable stress when in use. Now reinsert the pads you shaped earlier against the "body side" of each horn, leaving the 2" tail of the strap to the outside (that is, away from the wearer's body). Gently sew the pads in place (longest stitch and softest presser foot setting) by stitching directly through the pad one-half way back from its front end (Fig. 16-29). ("Walk" the machine by advancing the flywheel with your hand if necessary.)

Slide the waist belt buckles you have purchased into place on the webbing and try the rig around your waist. There should be no size problem if the waist belt is slightly too large even with the buckles in closest setting. When the sleeping bag compartment is filled, the horns will stand out from the body and the waistbelt will become snug.

Locating and Affixing the Shoulder Strap Leather Patch

Stuff some bulky items into the sleeping bag compartment and the two vertical chambers of the pack. Strap the waistbelt on and pin the shoulder straps approximately in position. Tug downward slightly on the pack to simulate a loaded condition. With chalk, mark a point on the back piece centerline level with the shoulders. Move the pinned upper ends of the shoulder straps until the fit is

BEFORE FOLDING:

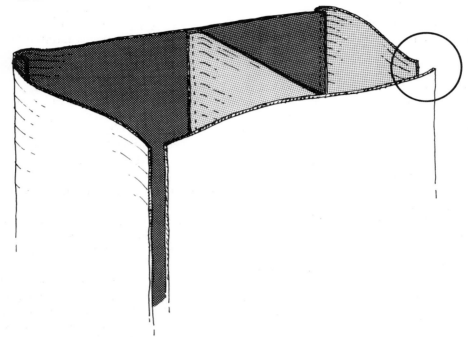

AFTER FOLDING:

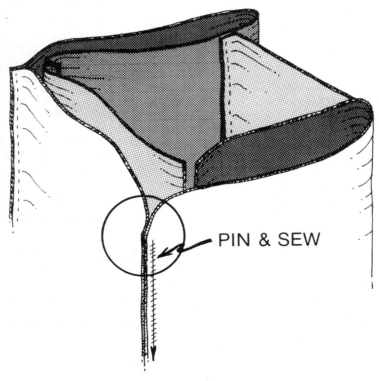

PIN & SEW

Figure 16-24

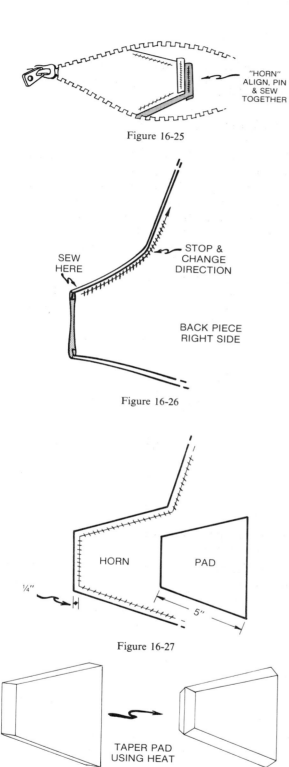

Figure 16-25

Figure 16-26

SEW HERE

STOP & CHANGE DIRECTION

BACK PIECE RIGHT SIDE

Figure 16-27

HORN

PAD

¼"

5"

Figure 16-28

TAPER PAD USING HEAT

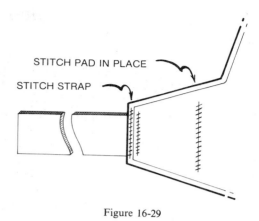

STITCH PAD IN PLACE

STITCH STRAP

Figure 16-29

satisfactory, then place a definite chalk mark. If you intend the pack to be worn by more than one person, repeat this marking procedure for each person.

Center the 3" × 5" leather patch on the mark you've located. You may adjust the patch size to accommodate other users of the pack or use two or more patches. Hand-stitch the leather patch in place through both front pieces with doubled heavy duty Dacron and cotton thread using a running stitch, backstitch, or overcast stitch, if you have the patience. (Note: A triangular tipped leather hand needle and thimble are helpful, but a better trick is to use a triangular-tip "leather" sewing machine needle in the machine to pierce the leather all around the edge with no thread in the needle before hand-sewing. Go slowly if the leather is thick or stiff and use a needle at least as large as that you have chosen for the hand sewing.) Place a mark on the leather piece indicating the shoulder height.

Inserting the Back Padding

(Note: These pads may be left out, at the expense of some back discomfort if hard items are carried against the body. They stiffen the pack but make it harder to roll or fold when empty. Their weight is approximately one-and-a-half ounces.) From a piece of bluefoam cut two padding pieces to the shape shown in Fig. 16-30. If you have made

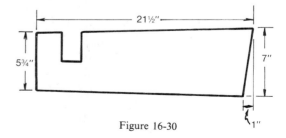

21½"

5¾"

7"

1"

Figure 16-30

123

significant alteration in the size of the pack, change the padding piece size accordingly. Note that the pad's tops are two full inches below the raw fabric edges. Check the pad size carefully against the front piece to determine the patch cut-out position. Use the first pad as a pattern for the second pad.

Taper the edges of the pads all around on both surfaces with a heated nail or soldering iron. Use caution because bluefoam burns and the melted edge is sticky and very hot. Provide ventilation.

Now remove the stitching holding the two front pieces together at the top raw edges. Roll the lower end of one pad and slide it into the space between the two front pieces past the leather patch stitching. Use a yardstick to unroll the pad and tuck it into the corners. Be certain it fits flat and is not puckered; remove and trim if required. When the second pad is in place to your satisfaction, machine-stitch the top edges of the back pieces together again.

With the punch provided in your grommetting kit and/or a hot rod held in a pliers, punch and heat-sear two holes through the leather patch and both back pieces. Locate each hole 2″ from the patch centerline and 1-1/2″ below its top edge. Position a washered grommet in each hole, smooth side out, and hammer it in firmly. Repeat this as required to locate the shoulder strap anchor points for other users of the pack.

Finishing the Bag Top Edge

Trim the top raw edges of front, back, and side pieces if necessary to even them. Fold the raw edge down 1″ to the wrong side and pin all around. Fold the vertical seam allowances away from the side pieces. Sew this hem in place close to the raw edge and again close to the fold. Eight size 0 or 1/4″ grommets are to be located in this rim fold. Locate four of them on the seam allowances of the front side and back side seams as shown in Fig. 16-31.

Place two more grommets on the front piece and two on the rear piece at points equidistant between those at

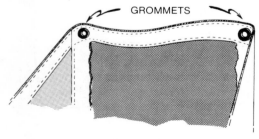

GROMMETS

Figure 16-31

the seams. Use the punch provided with the grommetting kit or a nail or rod heated in a flame to make the holes. Heat the hole edges, then hammer in the grommets through all thicknesses.

Making the Bag Top Flap

Fold the short sides of the rectangular flap piece 1/4″ toward the wrong side. Pin and sew 1/8″ from the folded edges. Repeat for the long sides. Next fold the short sides 1″ toward the wrong side to create drawstring sleeves. Pin and sew over the edge seams (Fig. 16-32).

Align the pack bag front edge with one long side of the flap piece right sides together and mark the grommet locations on the flap piece. Punch or melt holes through the flap piece at these marks and grommet. Using a cord-threading tool, insert a 40″ piece of 1/8″ nylon cord into each of the sleeves along the short sides of the top flap. Secure one end of each cord close to the corresponding grommet by sewing over the cord and sleeve several times.

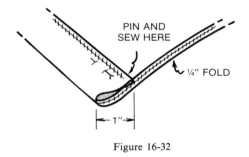

PIN AND SEW HERE

¼″ FOLD

1″

Figure 16-32

Preparing the Fastenings

Four clevis pins with lock rings are needed to complete the bag construction. At the two upper shoulder strap anchor points each clevis pin must fit through the three grommets; hauling loop, shoulder strap, and leather patch anchor point, with a minimum of "play." A heavy load and the impact loading on a loose fitting pin might bend the lock ring. The solution lies in cutting down a standard size aluminum clevis pin to 1/2″ shaft length (check this, as your grommets may differ) and drilling a 3/32″ to 5/32″ hole at a distance of 1/8″ from the sawn end. Both of these operations can easily be accomplished with hand tools in about five minutes per clevis pin. A tape-wrapped hacksaw blade will work fine for the cutting, if you have no hacksaw (Fig. 16-33).

The second pair of clevis pins pass through only two grommets: the center two of the top flap and bag edge.

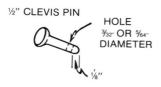

½" CLEVIS PIN

HOLE
³⁄₃₂" OR ⁵⁄₆₄"
DIAMETER

⅛"

Figure 16-33

They suffer little stress and serve only to hold the flap in position. I suggest that you make these two clevis pins to the dimensions required for the shoulder strap pins. They can be considered reserves in case the pins or lock rings holding the shoulder straps should be lost or bent, and they will function adequately in holding the flap in place.

Details of Final Assembly

Attach the top flap with two clevis pins in the center pair of holes so that the wrong side of the top flap edge lies against the right side of the grommetted upper edge of the pack bag back piece.

Tie a "figure eight" knot (see Chapter 2) in one end of the 3/16" or 1/8" cord 15" long. Insert the unknotted end of the cord through the wrong side of the grommet at the right-hand side of the front piece upper edge as in Fig. 16-34. Next thread the cord through the wrong side of the grommet at the right-hand edge of the top flap. Tie another "figure eight" knot snug against this second grommet so that it holds the flap and bag edge together. Thread the cord end through the next grommet, the first on the back piece, from right side to wrong side, then through the next grommet wrong side to right side. Now insert the cord end through a cord-locking device.

Repeat the above steps with a second piece of cord

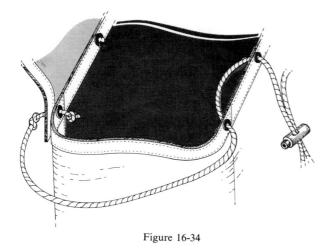

Figure 16-34

through the left-hand series of grommets, then tie a single overhand knot with both cord ends (Fig. 16-35).

Two cord lock devices must now be attached at the lace loops sewn into the pocket seams. Insert the lace loop through the simple holes (non-locking) near the base of the device (Fig. 16-36). Open the loop and pull it over the entire cordlock, then pull the cordlock snug.

Insert the cords protruding from the top flap sleeves into the locking holes in the cordlocks, then tie a simple overhand knot in the free end of each cord to prevent its coming loose.

Now insert a clevis pin through the right side of one end of the hauling loop, then through the wrong side of the grommetted end of a shoulder strap and finally into the right side of the leather patched anchor point (Fig. 16-37). Slip a lock ring through the hole in the clevis pin end. Repeat for the other side.

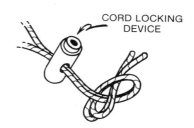

CORD LOCKING
DEVICE

Figure 16-35

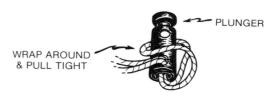

PLUNGER

WRAP AROUND
& PULL TIGHT

Figure 16-36

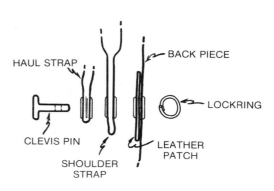

HAUL STRAP

BACK PIECE

LOCKRING

CLEVIS PIN

SHOULDER
STRAP

LEATHER
PATCH

Figure 16-37

125

Slide the lower shoulder strap web sections through the tabler buckles attached to the padded upper shoulder straps. Slip the waist belt buckle in place on its web strap (left hand side).

Now stuff the pack full of fluffy things. A sleeping bag would be appropriate for the sleeping bag compartment, down or Dacron jackets, knit clothing, pillows, etc. for the upper sections. Admire it.

Try the pack on to adjust waist and shoulder straps. The padded hip strap sections should contact the protruding "hip bones" in the front. The shoulder straps should leave their upper anchor points horizontally, or nearly so. The pack's weight (at least when the load exceeds twenty to twenty-five pounds) should rest largely on the "sacral shelf," the upper section of the posterior from below the vertical section of the backbone in the lumbar region to the top of the tail bone. The hip belt and shoulder straps are intended to keep the pack's weight forward over this region as well as support a small portion of the weight.

When your new pack fits to your satisfaction, slip it off and admire it some more. Pat yourself on the back for doing such a good job and for saving $30 to $50 to boot! Then get out the catalogs and the maps and guidebooks. Gather the family together or call a friend and pick a route. Buy some food with your savings, pack your newly-made gear, and have a nice trip.

Appendix I

Suppliers and Kit-Makers

(Patterns without kits indicated by*)

Altra, Inc.
3645 Pearl
Boulder, Colorado 80301

Calico Kits
1275 S. Sherman
Longmont, Colorado 80501

Collins Sport & Trail Patterns*
P. O. Box 99757
San Diego, California 92109

Country Ways
3500 Highway
Minnetonka, Minnesota 55343

Eastern Mountain Sports
1041 Commonwealth Ave.
Boston, Massachusetts 02215

Frostline
Frostline Circle
Denver, Colorado 80241

Holubar
P. O. Box 7
Boulder Colorado 80302

Makit
P. O. Box 571
Whittier, California 90608

Plain Brown Wrapper
2055 West Amherst Ave.
Inglewood, Colorado 80110

Recreational Equipment, Inc.*
P. O. Box Z1685
Seattle, Washington 98111

Sun Down
2700 W. Highland Dr.
Burnsville, Minnesota 55337

Timberline East, Inc.
144 Moody St.
Waltham, Massachusetts 02154

Appendix II

General Materials Suppliers

(Fabrics, Hardware, Tools, Etc.)

Brookstone
127 Vose Farm Road
Peterborough, N. H. 03458

Esp. Grommet Tools

Country Ways
(see Appendix I)

Esp. Polarguard

Eastern Mountain Sports
(see Appendix I)

Esp. Fiberfill II/Ripstop Bat

Early Winters
300 Queen Anne Ave., N.
Seattle, Wash. 98109

Esp. Gore-Tex

Frostline
(see Appendix I)

Makit
(see Appendix I)

Morsan Canvas Products
810 Route 17
Paramus, N. J.

Esp. Pole Sections

Recreational Equipment, Inc.
(see Appendix I)

Esp. Gore-Tex

Sierra Designs
247 Fourth St.
Oakland, Ca. 94607

Skihut (Trailwise)
P. O. Box 309
1615 University Ave.
Berkeley, Ca. 94701

Appendix III

Fabric Suppliers

All of the above General Suppliers handle standard backpacking fabrics at retail prices. You may want to investigate some unusual fabrics available at this sailmaker's supply:

Howe and Bainbridge
816 Production Place
Newport Beach, Ca. 92660

If you plan to make a few to several larger projects, you might search the yard goods section of your nearest big city yellow pages for a wholesale outlet. Some require a minimum order of as much as $50, but offer light ripstop at a $1.50 per yard or less—which is a 50% saving—or more! One such supplier in the Los Angeles area is:

United Textiles
761 N. Spring
Los Angeles, Ca.
(Minimum order $50; mail orders accepted)